Gdansk T
Guide 2024

A Comprehensive Journey through Enchanting Alleys, Historic Wharfs, and Cultural Wonders of Poland's Coastal Gem

Robert D. Richmond

Copyright © Robert D. Richmond 2024

All rights reserved. No part of this publication may be reproduced, distributed, or transmitted in any form or by any means, including photocopying, recording, or other electronic or mechanical methods, without the prior written permission of the publisher, except in the case of brief quotations embodied in critical reviews and certain other noncommercial uses permitted by copyright law.

SCAN THE QR CODE USING YOUR DEVICE TO GAIN ACCESS TO MORE OF MY BOOKS

TABLE OF CONTENTS

MAP OF GDANSK 6

INTRODUCTION 7

    Brief History of Gdańsk 11

    Fun facts and FAQs 14

    Why Visit Gdańsk? 24

CHAPTER 1: PLANNING YOUR TRIP 27

    Visa and Entry Requirements 27

    Best Time to visit 29

    Explore Gdańsk: A 5-Day Itinerary 32

    Budgeting and Currency 36

    Language and Local Customs 39

CHAPTER 2: GETTING TO GDANSK 43

    How to Get There 43

CHAPTER 3: GETTING AROUND 53

    Transportation in Gdansk 53

    Taxis and Ride-Sharing 56

    Renting a Car 59

Biking and Walking 61

CHAPTER 4: ACCOMMODATION 63

Where to Stay 63

CHAPTER 5: TOP ATTRACTIONS 77

Old Town Square 77

Mary's Basilica 79

Gdansk Crane 81

Westerplatte 84

Solidarity Centre 87

Oliwa Cathedral 89

Gdansk Shipyards 91

Amber Museum 93

CHAPTER 6: CULTURAL EXPERIENCES 97

Museums and Galleries 97

Theatres and Performing Arts 104

Music and Festivals 113

Local Cuisine and Culinary Experiences 115

CHAPTER 7: SHOPPING IN GDANSK 121

Markets and Bazaars 121

Unique Souvenirs 132

Fashion and Local Design 135

Shopping Districts 137

CHAPTER 8: NIGHTLIFE AND ENTERTAINMENT
.... 139

Bars and Pubs 139

Nightclubs 144

Live Music Venues 149

CHAPTER 9: DAY TRIPS FROM GDANSK 153

Sopot 153

Gdynia 156

Malbork Castle 159

Kashubian Switzerland 162

CHAPTER 10: OUTDOOR ACTIVITIES 167

Beaches and Waterfront 167

Parks and Gardens 170

Boating and Water Sports 176

Hiking and Nature Trails 179

CHAPTER 11: PRACTICAL INFORMATION 181

Emergency Contacts 181

Healthcare and Safety 183

Wi-Fi and Connectivity 185

Local Laws and Customs 188

CHAPTER 12: LOCAL EVENTS AND FESTIVALS 191

Annual Events Calendar 191

CHAPTER 13: SUSTAINABLE TRAVEL TIPS 195

Eco-Friendly Practices 195

Responsible Tourism Initiatives 198

CONCLUSION 201

MAP OF GDANSK

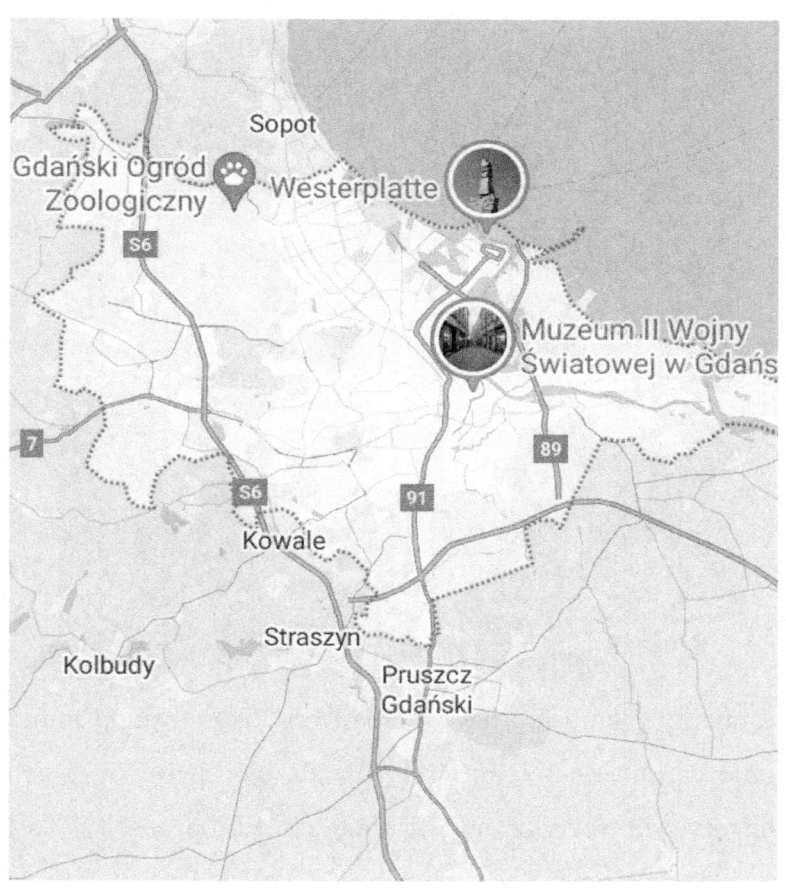

INTRODUCTION

Embarking on a journey to Gdansk is like stepping into a time capsule that effortlessly blends the charm of a rich history with the vibrancy of a modern European city. As I found myself wandering through the cobbled streets of Old Town, I couldn't help but marvel at the tales echoing from every corner – tales of maritime glory, architectural splendour, and the resilient spirit of a city that has witnessed centuries unfold.

Picture this: a cityscape adorned with medieval facades, where the scent of amber wafts through the air, and the rhythmic clatter of horse-drawn carriages adds a nostalgic soundtrack to your exploration. Gdansk, a jewel nestled along the Baltic Sea, welcomed me with open arms and a promise of discovery.

My journey began with the fascinating history that permeates Gdansk's every nook and cranny. The Old Town Square, a masterpiece frozen in time, unravelled stories of Hanseatic League trade routes and the towering elegance of St. Mary's Basilica. The medieval architecture, with its intricate details and pastel hues, transported me to an era where each building whispered secrets of bygone days.

The Gdansk Crane, standing proud on the waterfront, told tales of a bustling port and maritime prowess. As I stood there, absorbing the panoramic view of the Motlawa River, I couldn't help but appreciate the seamless blend of Gdansk's maritime past and its contemporary, lively present.

But Gdansk is more than just historical landmarks; it's a city that pulsates with cultural vibrancy. The Solidarity Centre, a symbol of resilience and freedom, resonates with the echoes of the shipyard workers' movement that changed the course of history. The Oliwa Cathedral, with its awe-inspiring organ concerts, offers a melodic interlude to your exploration, creating a harmonious fusion of spirituality and cultural richness.

As dusk settled over the city, I found myself immersed in the eclectic nightlife of Gdansk. The amber-lit streets came alive with the melodies of street performers, the laughter spilling from lively pubs, and the energetic beats echoing from nightclubs. Gdansk, it seemed, had mastered the art of balancing its historical grandeur with a modern, dynamic spirit.

Venturing beyond the city limits led me to discover the treasures nestled in Gdansk's surroundings. Sopot, a charming seaside resort, and Gdynia, a bustling port city, offered delightful day trips. The majestic Malbork Castle, a short journey away, stood as a testament to the medieval grandeur of the Teutonic Knights.

Gdansk is not just a destination; it's an immersive experience, a sensory journey through time, culture, and natural beauty. Join me as we delve into the heart of this enchanting city, uncovering its hidden gems, savouring its culinary delights, and immersing ourselves in the captivating rhythm of Gdansk. Through these pages, let the spirit of exploration guide you, and may Gdansk unfold its magic before your very eyes. Welcome to a city that invites you to be a part of its living history.

Brief History of Gdańsk

With its Old Town's cobblestones echoing tales that span centuries, Gdansk, tucked away along the Baltic Sea, is a monument to the tenacity of time. Come along with me as we explore the fascinating history of Gdansk and untangle its intricate fabric.

The Slavic tribes used Gdansk as a fishing town in the early medieval era, according to its historical accounts. Situated at the intersection of profitable trade routes, it developed into a thriving trading centre throughout time. The foundation of the strong commercial confederation known as the Hanseatic League in the fourteenth century is closely linked to the history of the city.

Gdansk prospered as an essential component of this commercial network, promoting economic success and cross-cultural interchange at the height of the Hanseatic period. Encircled by merchant homes that exhibited the riches and architectural excellence of the city, the famous Old Town Square became a centre of business.

Gdansk had its "Golden Age" in the 16th and 17th centuries when it saw revolutionary advancements and a thriving cultural environment. During this time, Gdansk was home to well-known individuals, including philosopher Arthur Schopenhauer and astronomer Johannes Hevelius. Magnificent buildings, such as the colossal St. Mary's Basilica, which remains a testimony to Gothic design, were built by the wealthy merchant elite of the city.

During the 20th century, Gdansk was at the centre of important historical developments. The Solidarity movement, spearheaded by Lech Walesa, originated at the

Gdansk Shipyards and was instrumental in bringing down the Iron Curtain. As a living tribute to the victory of the human spirit and the struggle for freedom, the Solidarity Center is still standing today.

Gdansk saw the devastation of World War II, with a large portion of its historic centre left to ruins. Nonetheless, the city launched an incredible rehabilitation project, painstakingly bringing its architectural treasures, including the Green Gate and the Gdansk Crane, back to their former splendour.

Gdansk now combines the vibrant energy of the modern era with its rich history. Once a thriving port, the city's waterfront is now a charming mix of old-world elegance and dynamic cultural venues. Rich layers to the cultural fabric of the city are added by museums like the Amber Museum, which honours Gdansk's nautical heritage and its amber commerce.

Every step we take reveals a new chapter in this fascinating story as we make our way through the old squares and alleyways of Gdansk. Turning pages and immersing yourself in the extraordinary narrative of a city that has endured the test of time is encouraged as Gdansk demonstrates how to adapt while maintaining its cultural legacy. Welcome to Gdansk, where historical secrets are spoken from every stone, and every nook tells a tale.

Fun facts and FAQs

Fun Facts

1. **Amber Capital:** Gdansk is often referred to as the "World Capital of Amber," as it has a rich tradition of amber trade and boasts the Amber Museum within its historic walls.
2. **Historical Trading Hub:** Gdansk was a key member of the Hanseatic League, a medieval trade alliance that greatly influenced the economic development of Northern Europe.
3. **Longest Brick Church:** St. Mary's Basilica in Gdansk is considered the world's largest brick church, showcasing impressive Gothic architecture and a stunning interior.
4. **Birthplace of Solidarity:** The Solidarity movement, a significant force in the collapse of communism in Eastern Europe, was born in the Gdansk Shipyards, led by Lech Walesa.

5. **City of Canals:** Gdansk features a network of picturesque canals reminiscent of Venice, adding to the city's unique charm.
6. **Copernicus' Hometown:** The renowned astronomer Nicolaus Copernicus had strong ties to Gdansk, as he studied at the local university before making groundbreaking discoveries.
7. **Green Gate Symbolism:** The Green Gate in Gdansk's Old Town, despite its name, is not actually green. It is a beautiful, richly adorned structure that once served as the formal residence for Polish monarchs.
8. **Motlawa Riverfront:** The waterfront along the Motlawa River is a lively area with colourful buildings, charming cafes, and bustling activity, making it a perfect spot for a stroll.
9. **Neptune's Fountain:** Gdansk boasts the impressive Neptune's Fountain, a symbol of the city's maritime history, located in the heart of Old Town.
10. **Famous Shipyard:** The Gdansk Shipyards gained global attention as the birthplace of the Solidarity

movement and played a crucial role in the downfall of communism in Poland.

11. **Gothic Beauty:** The medieval Gdansk Crane, a symbol of the city, is a massive wooden structure that was once used for loading and unloading cargo from ships.
12. **Long Market:** Dlugi Targ, or Long Market, is a bustling street in Gdansk's Old Town, lined with colourful houses and featuring numerous shops, restaurants, and cafes.
13. **City Gates:** Gdansk is known for its well-preserved city gates, including the iconic Golden Gate, which served as a grand entrance to the Old Town.
14. **Multi-Cultural Heritage:** Over the centuries, Gdansk has been influenced by various cultures, reflecting its diverse architectural styles and cultural traditions.
15. **World War II Ruins:** Despite extensive damage during World War II, Gdansk meticulously reconstructed its historic sites, allowing visitors to experience the city's rich history.

16. **Street of Royal Way:** The Royal Way, a historic route in Gdansk, takes you through the most prominent parts of the Old Town, passing by important landmarks.
17. **Beautiful Gardens:** Oliwa Park and the Oliwa Cathedral Gardens provide serene green spaces where visitors can relax and enjoy nature.
18. **Lighthouse in the City:** Gdansk is home to a unique urban lighthouse, the Westerplatte Lighthouse, providing a maritime touch within the city limits.
19. **Kashubian Tradition:** Gdansk is located in the Kashubia region and is known for its unique Kashubian language and cultural heritage.
20. **Longest Wooden Pier:** Sopot, a neighbouring town, boasts the longest wooden pier in Europe, offering stunning views of the Baltic Sea.
21. **European Solidarity Centre:** A modern museum, the European Solidarity Centre, chronicles the history of the Solidarity movement and the struggle for workers' rights.

22. **City of Museums:** Gdansk features numerous museums, including the National Maritime Museum and the World War II Museum, offering in-depth insights into its history.
23. **Teutonic Knights' Influence:** Malbork Castle, a short trip from Gdansk, was once the headquarters of the Teutonic Knights and is now a UNESCO World Heritage Site.
24. **Amber Clock in Old Town:** Gdansk's Old Town is adorned with the Amber Clock, a unique timepiece that incorporates amber into its design.
25. **Artistic Street Murals:** Gdansk embraces street art, with vibrant murals adorning walls across the city, adding a contemporary flair to its historic ambience.

Frequently Asked Questions (FAQs)

1. **What is the best time to visit Gdansk?**

The best time to visit Gdansk is during the summer months, from June to August when the weather is mild and outdoor activities are in full swing.

2. **How can I get to Gdansk from the airport?**

Gdansk Lech Walesa Airport is well-connected by public transport, taxis, and car rentals. There are also shuttle services available.

3. **Is English widely spoken in Gdansk?**

Yes, English is commonly spoken in Gdansk, especially in tourist areas, hotels, and restaurants.

4. **What are the must-visit attractions in Gdansk's Old Town?**

St. Mary's Basilica, Gdansk Crane, Neptune Fountain, and the Artus Court are must-visit attractions in Gdansk's Old Town.

5. **Are there any day trips from Gdansk worth exploring?**

Yes, Sopot, Gdynia, Malbork Castle, and Kashubian Switzerland are popular day trip destinations from Gdansk.

6. Where can I experience Gdansk's nightlife?

The Long Market and Długi Targ offer a vibrant nightlife scene with numerous bars, pubs, and nightclubs.

7. How can I explore Gdansk on a budget?

Opt for budget accommodations, use public transportation, and enjoy affordable local eateries for a budget-friendly experience.

8. What is the significance of the Gdansk Shipyards?

The Gdansk Shipyards played a crucial role in the Solidarity movement, contributing to the fall of communism in Poland.

9. Can I use public transportation to explore Gdansk?

Yes, Gdansk has an efficient public transportation system, including buses and trams, making it easy to explore the city.

10. Is Gdansk family-friendly?

Yes, Gdansk offers family-friendly attractions, parks, and activities suitable for all ages.

11. Where can I try traditional Polish cuisine in Gdansk?

Head to the Long Market and the Old Town for a variety of restaurants offering traditional Polish dishes.

12. How far is Gdansk from Warsaw, and how can I travel between the two cities?

Gdansk is approximately 3 hours away from Warsaw by train, making it a convenient option for travellers.

13. Are there any cultural events or festivals in Gdansk throughout the year?

Yes, Gdansk hosts various cultural events and festivals, such as the St. Dominic's Fair and the Gdansk Shakespeare Festival.

14. What is the significance of amber in Gdansk?

Gdansk has a rich amber trade history, and the Amber Museum showcases the importance of this gemstone in the city's culture.

15. Are there any beaches in Gdansk?

Yes, Gdansk boasts beautiful beaches along the Baltic Sea, with Stogi Beach being a popular choice.

16. Can I take a boat tour in Gdansk?

Yes, boat tours are available on the Motlawa River, providing scenic views of the city and its waterfront.

17. Are there any historical walking tours in Gdansk?

Absolutely! Gdansk offers various guided walking tours, allowing you to explore its history and architecture on foot.

18. How can I learn more about Gdansk's maritime history?

Visit the Maritime Museum or take a tour of the Gdansk Crane to delve into the city's maritime heritage.

19. Is Gdansk LGBTQ+ friendly?

Yes, Gdansk is generally LGBTQ+ friendly, with a welcoming atmosphere and LGBTQ+ events.

20. Can I use credit cards in Gdansk?

Yes, credit cards are widely accepted in Gdansk, but it's advisable to carry some Polish złoty for smaller establishments.

21. What are some souvenirs to buy in Gdansk?

Amber jewellery, traditional Polish pottery, and local crafts make excellent souvenirs from Gdansk.

22. Are there any green spaces in Gdansk for relaxation?

Yes, Oliwa Park and Plac Zebran Ludowych are serene green spaces for relaxation and picnics.

23. Can I visit Gdansk in winter?

Yes, Gdansk is enchanting in winter, with festive decorations, Christmas markets, and a cosy atmosphere.

24. How can I explore Gdansk by bike?

Gdansk is bike-friendly, with bike rental services available and dedicated bike paths for exploration.

25. What safety precautions should I take in Gdansk?

Gdansk is generally safe, but it's advisable to be cautious of pickpockets in crowded areas and adhere to basic safety practices.

Why Visit Gdańsk?

As a witness to the indescribable allure of Gdańsk, I can only convey the magic that this city weaves through its cobbled streets, historic landmarks, and vibrant spirit. Allow me to be your guide, sharing the joy and wonder that awaits you in this Baltic gem.

Gdańsk is not merely a destination; it is a captivating journey through time. As you stroll through the heart of the

Old Town, it's as if the very stones beneath your feet whisper tales of medieval grandeur, Hanseatic trade, and the resilience of a city that has withstood the tests of history. The architectural marvels of St. Mary's Basilica and the Gdańsk Crane stand as living testaments to the city's rich past, each brick resonating with stories that have shaped its identity.

The warmth of Gdańsk extends beyond its historic facades. The city's people, with their welcoming smiles and open hearts, make you feel like a part of their narrative. Engage with locals in the bustling Long Market, where centuries-old traditions meet the vibrancy of modern life. Sample traditional pierogi or savour the distinct taste of locally brewed beer while absorbing the lively atmosphere that permeates every corner.

Gdańsk is a city that has embraced its tumultuous history and transformed it into a source of pride. The Gdańsk Shipyards, once a crucible of political revolution during the Solidarity movement, now stand as a symbol of triumph and the enduring spirit of its people. The Solidarity Centre, with its interactive exhibits, paints a vivid picture of a city that dared to dream of freedom.

For those seeking tranquillity, Gdańsk's waterfront offers a peaceful retreat. Gaze upon the amber-hued sunsets, explore the Maritime Museum, or embark on a leisurely boat tour along the Motława River. The city's beaches, with their golden sands along the Baltic Sea, provide a serene escape for those who wish to unwind.

In Gdańsk, every corner is an invitation to explore, every building a chapter in a living story. Whether you're captivated by history, enchanted by culture, or simply in search of a city that feels like a warm embrace, Gdańsk welcomes you with open arms. So, embark on this journey, let the spirit of Gdańsk envelop you, and allow yourself to be swept away by the enchantment that awaits in this extraordinary city by the sea.

CHAPTER 1: PLANNING YOUR TRIP

Visa and Entry Requirements

EU citizens

- You can enter Poland and Gdańsk visa-free with a valid passport or national ID card.
- You have the option to remain for a maximum of 90 days within a 180-day timeframe.

Non-EU citizens

- You will generally need a Schengen visa to enter Poland and Gdańsk.
- There are a few exceptions, such as if you are a citizen of a country that has a visa-free agreement with Poland or if you are a permanent resident of another Schengen country.
- You can apply for a Schengen visa at the Polish consulate or embassy in your home country.

Types of Schengen visas

- There are different types of Schengen visas, depending on the purpose and duration of your stay.

- The most common type of visa for short-term stays (up to 90 days) is the tourist visa.
- If you are planning to stay for longer than 90 days, you will need to apply for a different type of visa, such as a business visa, study visa, or work visa.

Documents required for a Schengen visa application

The required documents for a Schengen visa application may vary, but they typically include:

- A completed visa application form
- Two passport-sized photos
- Your valid passport
- Proof of travel health insurance
- Evidence of ample financial resources to support your duration of stay in Poland.
- Proof of accommodation in Gdańsk

Best Time to visit

Choosing the best time to visit Gdańsk depends on what kind of experience you're looking for:

Warm weather and outdoor activities

- **May-September:** These are the warmest months, with average temperatures between 15°C (59°F) and 20°C (68°F). July and August are the peak months, offering the best chance for sunshine and swimming, but they are also the busiest and most expensive. June and September can be good compromises for slightly lower temperatures and crowds.

Fewer crowds and lower prices

- **April-May:** Temperatures start to become pleasant, and you'll see fewer tourists and lower prices compared to peak season. Nevertheless, the climate remains uncertain, featuring sporadic instances of rainfall.
- **September-October:** The weather gets cooler, but it's still comfortable for sightseeing and outdoor

activities. Prices are lower, and you'll have the city practically to yourself.

Festivals and events

- **St. Dominic's fair (June-July):** Gdańsk's biggest festival, with traditional food, music, and performances.
- **International Kite Festival (September):** Hundreds of colourful kites fill the sky over the beach.
- **Christmas Market (December):** Enjoy festive decorations, shopping, and traditional treats.

Other factors to consider

- **Rainfall:** July and August are the wettest months, so be prepared for rain showers.
- **Daylight hours:** The longest days are in June, with over 17 hours of daylight.
- **Accommodation and flights:** Prices are highest in peak season (July-August). Book well in advance if you're travelling during this time.

In summary:

- **May or September:** Best for pleasant weather and moderate crowds.

- **June-August:** Best for warm weather and outdoor activities, but expect crowds and higher prices.
- **April-May and September-October:** Good for budget travellers and those who prefer a quieter experience.

Explore Gdańsk: A 5-Day Itinerary

DAY 1: Exploring Gdańsk Old Town

- **MORNING:** Start your day by visiting the iconic Gdansk Old Town (Gdańsk Stare Miasto). Take a leisurely walk through the charming streets, admire the colourful buildings, and explore the historical landmarks. Grab breakfast at Główne Miasto Restauracja & Kawiarnia and enjoy some traditional Polish dishes.
- **AFTERNOON:** After lunch at Pod Żagli, continue your exploration of Gdańsk Old Town. Visit St. Mary's Basilica (Kościół Mariacki), a magnificent Gothic church, and learn about its rich history. Pause at Browar Piwna, a nearby brewery, and savour a revitalizing beer.
- **EVENING:** For dinner, head to Mechanika Samochodowego Smaku and savour delicious Polish cuisine. Afterwards, join a Gdansk Pub Crawl with Free Drinks to experience the vibrant nightlife of Gdańsk.

DAY 2: City Sights and Historical Tour

- **MORNING:** Start your day with a guided Gdańsk City Sights and History Guided Walking Tour to discover more about the city's fascinating history and landmarks. Indulge in a cup of coffee and a light morning meal at Miód Malina.
- **AFTERNOON:** After the tour, have lunch at Pierogarnia Mandu and indulge in traditional Polish dumplings. In the afternoon, take a Gdańsk City Cruise on Historical Polish Boat to admire the city from a different perspective.
- **EVENING:** For dinner, try the delicious seafood at Stylowa Restauracja Morska. Afterwards, enjoy a relaxing evening walk along the Motława River and savour the beautiful views.

DAY 3: Cultural and Museum Experience

- **MORNING:** Visit the Nicolaus Copernicus Museum (Muzeum Mikolaja Kopernika) to learn about the life and achievements of the famous astronomer. Indulge in a brief snack at Pivovar Gdańsk before resuming your exploration.

- **AFTERNOON:** Head to the Gdansk Stutthof Concentration Camp Regular Tour for a sobering and educational experience. Following the tour, indulge in a late lunch at Północ Południe, a renowned restaurant celebrated for its contemporary Polish culinary offerings.
- **EVENING:** Spend the evening at Gdańsk. Enjoy City Views and Delicious Food on the Top Floor, a rooftop restaurant with panoramic views of the city. Experience a gourmet dining affair amidst the breathtaking landscape.

DAY 4: Adventure and Fun

- **MORNING:** Start your day with an adrenaline-filled Gdansk Firearm Shooting Experience with Instructor. Subsequently, indulge in a swift meal at Krowarzywa, a vegan burger establishment.
- **AFTERNOON:** Experience extreme gun shooting at Gdansk Extreme Gun Shooting. Experience with Transfers and feel the thrill of handling different firearms. For a mid-afternoon meal, visit PiecNaSztramach and savour their delightful selection of Polish street cuisine.

- **EVENING:** Enjoy a scenic Gdańsk Sightseeing Cruise around the Old Town of Gdansk in the evening. For dinner, try the traditional Polish cuisine at Bulaj, a restaurant located by the waterfront.

DAY 5: Relaxation and Panoramic Views

- **MORNING:** Start your day by visiting Gdańsk Olivia Star Panoramic Views and Olivia Garden Dinner. Experience stunning cityscape panoramas from the vantage point of the observation deck. Grab breakfast at Jadalnia na wypasie and savour some delicious Polish pastries.
- **AFTERNOON:** Take a stroll along the sandy beaches of nearby Sopot, one of the adjacent cities. Enjoy a midday meal at La Sirena, a coastal dining establishment renowned for its delectable seafood offerings.
- **EVENING:** Return to Gdańsk and enjoy a relaxing dinner at MOTŁAWA, a restaurant with a beautiful view of the Motława River. End your trip with a visit to Filharmonia Restauracja, a restaurant located in the iconic Polish Baltic Philharmonic

building, and enjoy live music performances while savouring your meal.

Budgeting and Currency

Budgeting for your trip to Gdańsk

Gdańsk is a beautiful and relatively affordable city to visit. However, it's always helpful to have a budget in mind before you go. Here are some things to consider when budgeting for your trip:

- **Accommodation:** There are a variety of accommodation options in Gdańsk, from hostels and guesthouses to luxury hotels. Hostels can be as cheap as €10 per night, while guesthouses start at around €20 per night. Hotels can range from €50 to €200 or more per night.
- **Food:** Polish food is delicious and affordable. You can expect to pay around €5-€10 for a meal at a casual restaurant. If you're on a tight budget, you can also find plenty of street food and snacks for €1-€2.
- **Activities:** There are many free and cheap things to do in Gdańsk, such as exploring the Old Town, visiting the Maritime Museum, or relaxing on the

beach. If you want to do some paid activities, such as taking a boat trip or visiting a museum, expect to pay around €10-€20.
- **Transportation:** Getting around Gdańsk is easy and affordable. The city has a tram system that costs €1.50 per ticket. You can also buy a 24-hour pass for €6 or a 72-hour pass for €12. Taxis are also relatively cheap, with fares starting at around €5.

Here's a sample budget for a 3-day trip to Gdańsk for a solo traveller on a budget:
- **Accommodation:** €30/night x 3 nights = €90
- **Food:** €10/day x 3 days = €30
- **Activities:** €10/day x 3 days = €30
- **Transportation:** €5/day x 3 days = €15
- **Total:** €165

Of course, this is just a sample budget, and your actual expenses will vary depending on your travel style and preferences. But hopefully, it gives you a good starting point for planning your trip.

Currency in Gdańsk

The currency in Gdańsk is the Polish złoty (PLN). You can exchange your currency for złotys before you travel or at currency exchange offices in Gdańsk. There are also ATMs in Gdańsk where you can withdraw złotys from your bank account.

Here are some tips for saving money on currency exchange:

- Avoid exchanging currency at airports, train stations, and hotels, as they typically offer poor exchange rates.
- If you're bringing cash, bring euros or US dollars, as they are the most widely accepted currencies in Poland.
- Use a credit card or debit card with no foreign transaction fees.
- Consider using a travel money card, which can be loaded with złotys before you travel.

Language and Local Customs

Polish is the primary language spoken in Gdańsk, with Pomeranian, a regional dialect, spoken by some. While younger generations often have English proficiency, learning some basic Polish phrases will go a long way in your interactions with locals. Here are some helpful tips:

- **Essential phrases:** Hello (Dzień dobry), Goodbye (Do widzenia), Please (Proszę), Thank you (Dziękuję), You're welcome (Nie ma za co), Do you speak English? (Czy mówisz po angielsku?)
- **Pronunciation:** Many Polish consonants have different sounds than their English counterparts. "W" is pronounced like "v," "ł" is a soft "l," and "ó" is like a long "oo."
- **Non-verbal communication:** A nod and a smile can go a long way. Learning gestures like shaking hands to greet and thank you can also be helpful.

Local Customs in Gdańsk

Gdańsk has a rich history and traditions, manifested in its customs. Here are some to experience:

- **Amber jewellery:** Gdańsk is a world centre for amber, so browsing and acquiring a piece of amber jewellery is a must-do.
- **St. Dominic's Fair:** This annual summer fair (late July-mid August) showcases traditional crafts, food, and performances.
- **Neptune Fountain:** Throwing a coin into this iconic fountain brings good luck and ensures your return to Gdańsk.
- **Food and drink:** Try local specialities like pierogi (dumplings), kaszubska zupa (fish soup), and goldwasser (amber vodka liqueur).
- **Etiquette:** It's polite to address older people with "pan" (Mr.) and "pani" (Ms.). Offering your seat to the elderly is also appreciated.

Here are some additional things to keep in mind:

- **Tipping:** Tipping is not expected in Poland, but a small gratuity (5-10%) is appreciated for good service.
- **Smoking:** Smoking is banned in most public places, including restaurants and bars.

- **Public transportation:** Tickets for trams and buses should be validated before boarding.

CHAPTER 2: GETTING TO GDANSK

How to Get There

From Asia

By plane

This is the quickest and most convenient option, especially if you're flying from a major Asian city. Many airlines offer flights to Gdańsk Lech Wałęsa Airport (GDN), including LOT Polish Airlines, Lufthansa, KLM, Emirates, and Qatar Airways. You can also find connecting flights through European hubs like Amsterdam, Frankfurt, or Paris.

- **Flight time:** Varies depending on your origin city in Asia, but expect at least 12-15 hours for a flight with one layover.
- **Cost:** Prices can vary widely depending on the season, airline, and availability of deals. Generally, you can expect to pay between PLN 2,279 (around USD 500) and PLN 5,000 (around USD 1,100) for a round-trip flight from a major Asian city to Gdańsk.

By train

Taking the train from Asia to Gdańsk is a great option if you're looking for a more scenic and relaxed travel experience. However, it's also the slowest option and requires multiple connections. There are no direct trains from most Asian cities to Gdańsk, so you'll need to plan your route carefully. Some possible routes include:

- Beijing-Moscow-Berlin-Gdańsk
- Delhi-Moscow-Minsk-Warsaw-Gdańsk
- Tokyo-Vladivostok-Khabarovsk-Moscow-Gdańsk
- Travel time: This can take anywhere from 5 days to 2 weeks, depending on your route and connections.

Cost: Train tickets can be cheaper than flights, especially if you book in advance and travel during the off-season. However, you'll also need to factor in the cost of food, accommodation, and visas for any countries you transit through.

By bus

Taking a bus from Asia to Gdańsk is the most budget-friendly option, but it's also the slowest and least comfortable. Buses from most Asian cities to Gdańsk will require multiple connections and overnight journeys. This option is only really recommended if you're on a very tight budget or if you enjoy the challenge of overland travel.

- **Travel time:** This can take anywhere from 7 days to 3 weeks, depending on your route and connections.
- **Cost:** Bus tickets can be very cheap, often starting at around USD 100 for a one-way trip. However, you'll need to factor in the cost of food, accommodation, and visas for any countries you transit through.

By ferry

There are no direct ferries from Asia to Gdańsk, but you could take a ferry from one of the major Asian ports to a European port and then continue your journey by train or bus. This option is only really feasible if you're living near a major port in Asia and have plenty of time to travel.

- **Travel time:** Varies depending on your route and connections, but expect at least two weeks.
- **Cost:** It can be expensive, especially if you need to book a cabin on the ferry.

From North America

By plane: This is the quickest and most convenient option, but also the most expensive. Many airlines offer flights from major North American cities to Gdańsk Lech Wałęsa Airport (GDN), including:

- LOT Polish Airlines (from New York, Chicago, and Toronto)
- Lufthansa (from Chicago, Montreal)
- KLM Royal Dutch Airlines (from New York, Toronto)
- Air Canada (from Toronto)
- Scandinavian Airlines (from New York, Chicago)
- United Airlines (from Newark)

You can also find connecting flights through major European hubs like Frankfurt, Amsterdam, or Paris. Flight time will vary depending on your departure city, but most flights will take between 10 and 12 hours.

By train: This is a more scenic and affordable option, but it takes much longer than flying. There are no direct trains from North America to Gdańsk, so you would need to take a series of connecting trains. One possible route would be to take Amtrak to New York City, then take a British Airways flight to London Heathrow Airport. From there, you can take a Eurostar train to Paris, and then another train to Berlin. Finally, you can take a train from Berlin to Gdańsk. This journey would take about 48 hours.

By ferry: There are a few ferry companies that offer crossings from North America to Europe, but none of them go directly to Gdańsk. You could take a ferry from New York City to Bremerhaven, Germany, and then take a train to Gdańsk. This journey would take about seven days.

By bus: There are a few bus companies that offer long-distance journeys from North America to Europe, but none of them go directly to Gdańsk. You could take a bus from New York City to Berlin and then take a train to Gdańsk. This journey would take about seven days.

Regardless of the mode of transportation you select, it is advisable to make bookings for your tickets, particularly during peak seasons.

Here are some additional tips for getting to Gdańsk from North America:

- If you are flying, be sure to check the baggage restrictions of your airline.
- If you are taking the train, be sure to purchase your tickets in advance and print them out at home.

- If you are taking the ferry or bus, be sure to pack plenty of snacks and drinks.

From South America

By plane

This is the quickest and most convenient option, but also the most expensive. There are no direct flights from most South American cities to Gdańsk, so you will need to make a connection at a European or North American airport. Some possible flight itineraries include:

- São Paulo (GRU) to Gdańsk (GDN) with Lufthansa via Frankfurt (FRA): This is a popular option with good connections and service. Lufthansa is a member of Star Alliance, so you can earn miles on your flight if you are a member of a Star Alliance frequent flyer program.
- Buenos Aires (EZE) to Gdańsk (GDN) with LOT Polish Airlines via Warsaw (WAW): LOT Polish Airlines is the national airline of Poland, so they offer the most frequent flights between Warsaw and Gdańsk. They are also a member of Star Alliance.
- Bogotá (BOG) to Gdańsk (GDN) with KLM Royal Dutch Airlines via Amsterdam (AMS): KLM Royal

Dutch Airlines is a member of SkyTeam, so you can earn miles on your flight if you are a member of a SkyTeam frequent flyer program.

Other airlines that offer flights from South America to Gdańsk with connections include Air France, Iberia, and Alitalia.

By plane and train

You can also fly to a major European city such as London, Paris, or Frankfurt and then take a train to Gdańsk. This can be a cheaper option than flying directly to Gdańsk, but it will take longer. Some possible train routes include:

- London (LHR) to Gdańsk (GDN) via Berlin (BER): This is a popular route with several trains per day. The journey takes about 15 hours.
- Paris (CDG) to Gdańsk (GDN) via Berlin (BER): This route is similar to the London-Gdańsk route, but it takes a little longer (about 16 hours).
- Frankfurt (FRA) to Gdańsk (GDN): This is a direct train route that takes about 12 hours.

By ship

There are no regular passenger ships from South America to Europe, so this is not a practical option for most travellers. However, there are occasional cruises that sail from South America to Europe, and some of these cruises may make a stop in Gdańsk.

By car

Driving from South America to Gdańsk is a very long and challenging journey, and it is not recommended for most travellers. The trip would take several weeks or even months, and you would need to obtain visas for all of the countries you would be passing through.

Once you have decided on a mode of transportation, you can start booking your tickets. There are a number of websites and travel agents that can help you find the best deals on flights, trains, and cruises.

From Africa

By Plane

Direct flights: This is the quickest and most comfortable option, although often the most expensive. Several airlines offer direct flights from major African cities to Gdańsk Lech Wałęsa Airport (GDN). Here are some possibilities:

- **South Africa:** Ethiopian Airlines, Lufthansa, Swiss International Air Lines
- **Kenya:** KLM Royal Dutch Airlines, Qatar Airways

- **Nigeria:** LOT Polish Airlines, Turkish Airlines
- **Egypt:** LOT Polish Airlines, Turkish Airlines
- **Morocco:** Royal Air Maroc

Connecting flights: With more options available, connecting flights can be cheaper, though with longer travel times and layovers. Look for flights with reputable airlines like Lufthansa, KLM, Emirates, Turkish Airlines, etc., that offer convenient connections with African hubs like Addis Ababa, Cairo, Casablanca, or Doha.

By Train and Ferry

Trans-Saharan Railway: This adventurous option involves taking a train across the Sahara Desert, followed by ferry crossings in the Mediterranean Sea. While offering a unique experience, it requires significant planning and may not be the fastest or most reliable choice.

By Car

Driving: Technically possible, driving from Africa to Gdańsk would be an epic overland journey spanning thousands of kilometres, crossing multiple borders, and requiring extensive preparation and logistical planning. Not recommended for most travellers!

Additional factors to consider

- **Visa requirements:** Ensure you have the necessary visas for all countries you'll transit through and Gdańsk itself.
- **Travel time:** Direct flights can take around 13-15 hours while connecting flights or other modes of travel will significantly increase the journey time.
- **Cost:** Direct flights are typically the most expensive while connecting flights or overland options can be cheaper but may involve additional costs like visa fees, fuel, or ferry expenses.

CHAPTER 3: GETTING AROUND

Transportation in Gdansk

Gdansk offers several convenient transportation options for visitors, making it easy to explore the city and its surrounding areas. Here's a breakdown of your choices:

Public Transportation

- **Trams and Buses:** Gdansk has an extensive network of trams and buses operated by ZTM (Zespół Komunikacji Miejskiej w Gdańsku). Tickets are affordable and can be purchased at ticket machines, kiosks, or directly from the driver. Consider single-ride tickets for short trips or time tickets valid for 60 minutes, 24 hours, or longer, depending on your needs. The Gdansk Tourist Card also includes public transportation access and various discounts.

- **SKM Commuter Train:** This is the best choice for travelling between Gdansk, Sopot, and Gdynia. The trains run frequently and offer a quick and comfortable ride. Tickets are available for purchase from automated machines located at train stations.
- **Water Taxis:** A unique and scenic way to get around, especially between Gdansk Old Town and Westerplatte peninsula. Several companies offer water taxi services, and ticket prices vary depending on the route and operator.

Other Options

- **Taxis:** Taxis are readily available throughout the city and can be hailed on the street, ordered through phone apps, or at taxi stands. Metered fares are generally reasonable, but agree on the price before taking the ride.
- **Bicycles:** Gdansk is a bike-friendly city with dedicated lanes and bike rentals available in many

locations. Renting a bike is a great way to explore the city at your own pace and enjoy the fresh air.
- **Walking:** The Old Town and other central areas are best explored on foot, allowing you to experience the city's charming architecture and atmosphere.

Here are some additional tips for using transportation in Gdansk as a visitor:

- Download the JakDojade app for real-time public transportation information and route planning.
- Validate your ticket on trams and buses upon boarding.
- Be aware of pickpockets in crowded areas, especially on public transportation.
- Consider purchasing the Gdansk Tourist Card for discounted transportation and attractions.
- Most public transportation operates until late at night, so you shouldn't have trouble getting around even after dark.

Taxis and Ride-Sharing

Getting around Gdansk as a visitor is easy, thanks to the variety of taxi and ride-sharing options available. Here's a rundown of what you need to know:

Taxis

- **Licensed taxis:** Gdansk has many licensed taxi companies, which are the safest and most reliable option. They are easily recognizable by their official markings, usually a yellow license plate with a taxi company logo.
- **Hailing a taxi:** You can hail a taxi on the street or at designated taxi ranks, which are usually found near popular tourist spots like the Old Town Square and the Main Railway Station.
- **Ordering a taxi:** You can also call a taxi company directly or use their app to book a ride. Some popular taxi companies in Gdansk include City Taxi, AS Taxi, and Hallo Taxi Gdańsk.
- **Fares:** Taxi fares in Gdansk are metered and generally considered reasonable. The starting fare is around 7 PLN (1.60 USD), and the cost per kilometre is around 3 PLN (0.70 USD). You can

- always ask the driver for an estimate before you start your journey.
- **Tips:** Tipping taxi drivers in Gdansk is not mandatory, but it is appreciated. A small tip of around 5-10% of the fare is customary.

Ride-sharing

- **Uber:** Uber operates in Gdansk, so you can use your Uber app to book a ride. This can be a convenient option if you are familiar with Uber and prefer cashless payments.
- **Bolt:** Bolt is another popular ride-sharing app in Gdansk. It is often cheaper than Uber and offers a wider range of car types, including economy, comfort, and vans.
- **Free Now:** Free Now is another option for ride-sharing in Gdansk. It is a merger of the MyTaxi and Kapten apps, so you may have one of these apps already on your phone.

Here are some additional things to keep in mind when using taxis or ride-sharing in Gdansk:

- **Language:** Not all taxi drivers in Gdansk speak English, so it may be helpful to learn a few basic Polish phrases before you go.
- **Payment:** Most taxis and ride-sharing apps accept cash and credit cards.
- **Traffic:** Gdansk can experience traffic congestion, especially during peak hours. This can affect the time it takes to get to your destination, so be sure to factor this in when planning your trips.

Renting a Car

Renting a car in Gdansk as a visitor can be a great way to explore the city and its surroundings at your own pace. Here are a few things to keep in mind:

- **Requirements:** To rent a car in Poland, you must be at least 19 years old and have a valid driver's license held for at least one year. An International Driving Permit (IDP) is recommended, although not mandatory for EU/EEA citizens.
- **Rental companies:** There are many car rental companies in Gdansk, both international and local. Some popular options include Sixt, Europcar, PANEK Car Rental, and Global Rent a Car. You can compare prices and book your car online before you travel.
- **Pick-up and drop-off:** You can pick up your rental car at the airport, in the city centre, or at another convenient location. Most companies offer one-way rentals, so you can drop off your car in a different city if you like.
- **Insurance:** Be sure to check the insurance options included in your rental rate. You may want to

purchase additional insurance to cover theft, damage, and third-party liability.
- **Traffic:** Traffic in Gdansk can be congested, especially during peak hours. Make sure to allocate additional time for your travels.
- **Parking:** Parking in Gdansk can be difficult, especially in the city centre. Search for assigned parking spaces or designated car parks.
- **Driving tips:** Drivers in Poland drive on the right side of the road. The speed limit in built-up areas is 50 km/h (31 mph) and 90 km/h (56 mph) on motorways.

Here are a few additional tips for renting a car in Gdansk:
- Book your car in advance, especially if you are travelling during peak season.
- Carefully review the rental agreement prior to signing it.
- Make sure you understand the insurance coverage.
- Ask about any additional fees, such as one-way rental fees or young driver fees.
- Fill up the tank before you return the car.

Biking and Walking

Gdansk is a beautiful city in northern Poland that is perfect for exploring by bike or on foot. The city is relatively flat, making it easy to get around, and there are plenty of bike paths and pedestrian walkways to choose from.

Here are some tips for biking and walking in Gdansk as a visitor:

- **Rent a bike:** There are many places to rent bikes in Gdansk, including from the city's public bike-sharing system. You can also rent bikes from some hotels and tour operators.
- **Plan your route:** There are many different routes you can take when biking or walking in Gdansk. Some popular routes include the Motława Riverfront, the Old Town, and the Jelitkowo Beach. You can find maps of these routes online or at the tourist information office.
- **Be aware of traffic:** While Gdansk is a relatively bike-friendly city, it is still important to be aware of traffic. Be sure to obey all traffic laws and signals, and use the designated bike paths whenever possible.

- **Take your time:** Gdansk is a beautiful city, so take your time to explore it on foot or by bike. There are numerous captivating sights and activities to experience throughout the journey.

Here are some additional things to keep in mind when biking or walking in Gdansk:

- The weather in Gdansk can be variable, so be sure to dress in layers.
- Be sure to wear comfortable shoes that you can walk or bike in for long periods.
- Bring sunscreen and a hat, especially if you are going to be outside for a long time.
- Drink plenty of water, especially if it is hot or humid.
- Show consideration for the customs and culture of the local community.

CHAPTER 4: ACCOMMODATION

Where to Stay

PURO Gdansk Stare Miasto

- Address: Stagiewna 26, Gdansk 80-750 Poland
- Hotel Class: 4-Star Hotel
- Price per day: $103

Puro Gdansk is an urban haven tucked away in the centre of Gdansk, only 300 meters from the busy Long Market and 150 meters from the famous Green Gate. In addition to putting you in the middle of all the historical charm, this modern treasure also provides a sanctuary of contemporary luxury and convenience.

The Hotel invites visitors to a seamless fusion of luxury and technology with its streamlined design and attentive facilities. With a flat-screen TV, air conditioning, and an iPad, each room is a haven of tranquillity. A hairdryer and free toiletries are provided in the private bathrooms, which include refreshing showers and provide a luxurious stay.

The dedication to ensuring client happiness at Puro Gdansk extends beyond the room. A complementary assortment of hot drinks is waiting for you, a gesture that perfectly captures the Hotel's commitment to providing a cosy and welcoming environment. Our experience is made easier with express check-in and check-out options, a round-the-clock front desk, and flexible meeting spaces.

Puro Gdansk is a prime location for visitors who want to see Gdansk's rich historical tapestry because of its proximity to famous sites, including Artus Court and Main Town Hall. Discover the cultural treasure that is the National Museum, which is only 1.2 kilometres away and appeals to both history and art lovers.

Hilton Gdansk

- **Address: Targ Rybny 1, Gdansk 80-838 Poland**
- **Hotel Class: 5-Star Hotel**
- **Price per day: $110**

In the centre of Gdansk, the Hilton Gdansk welcomes you to a new age of elegance and refinement. A state-of-the-art sanctuary that skillfully combines modernity with the rich historical fabric of the city. With its unrivalled amenities, this gorgeous new Hotel in the heart of Gdansk proudly holds the title of the biggest meeting, incentive, conference, and exhibition venue.

Hilton Gdansk is well situated to complement the ancient architecture of Poland's main seaport, nestled along the lovely banks of the River Motlawa. Its modern architecture blends in well with Old Town's beauty, creating a smooth transition between the city's past and present.

Hilton Gdansk's prime location in the centre of Old Town puts you close to major commercial districts and well-known tourist destinations. Walk slowly along Mariacka Street, where quaint cafés and artisanal shops may be found along cobblestone walkways. Explore the European Solidarity Center's history of the Solidarity movement or bask in the splendour of St. Mary's Church, a magnificent example of Gothic architecture.

Radisson Blu Hotel, Gdansk

- **Address: Dlugi Targ 19 / Powroznicza, Gdansk 80-828 Poland**
- **Hotel Class: 5-Star Hotel**
- **Price per day: $108**

The Radisson Blu Hotel, with its alluring mix of modernity and charm, invites visitors as it is perched on the prestigious Long Market Street (Długi Targ) in the centre of Gdansk's historic Old Town. You are welcomed by a seamless blend of modern luxury and the ageless charm of the city's legendary heritage as soon as you enter this elegant refuge.

Gdansk's rich history may be explored via the Radisson Blu Hotel, which is well-situated next to the famous St. Mary's Church. A memorable stay is guaranteed from the minute you walk into the elegantly designed foyer. It is both luxurious and inviting, with modern design features that seamlessly blend in with the historic surroundings.

Enjoy the luxury of luxurious apartments and rooms with expansive views of the bustling Long Market. With facilities to satisfy even the most discriminating tourists, every area has been painstakingly created to provide a peaceful retreat. Savour the view of the city outside your window, sink into luxurious linen and feel the peace that characterizes a Radisson Blu stay.

Its dining venues demonstrate the Hotel's dedication to culinary quality. The Verres en Vers Restaurant offers a unique eating experience via the mix of local foods and foreign tastes, so indulge your palette with a gourmet adventure. Dining has become an art form because of the chic decor and careful service that elevate every meal.

Hanza Hotel

- **Address: Ul. Tokarska 6, Gdansk 80-888 Poland**
- **Hotel Class: 4-Star Hotel**
- **Price per day: $102**

Find a sanctuary of luxury and ease at Hotel Hanza, which is ideally situated between the famous Gdańsk Crane and the busy Main Town and just a short walk from the lively Długa Street. This well-situated Hotel provides quick access to Gdańsk's top attractions while engrossing you in a rich tapestry of cultural marvels.

The Second World War Museum is about 800 meters away, perfect for history buffs who want to immerse themselves in the moving stories of the past. The European Solidarity Centre, a monument to the city's revolutionary role in the struggle for independence, is only a 1.5-kilometer walk away.

The close vicinity to Forum Gdańsk, a shopping paradise with a multitude of your favourite brands and 31 cafés, bars, and restaurants, will thrill foodies and shopaholics alike. Hotel Hanza makes sure you're in the centre of everything, whether you're shopping or taking in the history of the city.

Hotel Almond Business & Spa

- **Address: Torunska 12, Gdansk 80-747 Poland**
- **Hotel Class: 4-Star Hotel**
- **Price per day: $119**

In the centre of Gdańsk, our four-star business and convention hotel welcomes you to an amazing refuge designed for the exceptional you. Our institution embraces elegance and maintains an intimate ambience, catering to those who expect the highest standards of quality, creativity, and comfort.

Our Hotel is a contemporary haven that was converted from a chocolate and marzipan factory, and it is located in the heart of Gdańsk. Its architecture is a tribute to architectural brilliance. This transformation effortlessly combines a unique and modern aesthetic with traditional beauty, capturing the essence of reinvention.

Providing an unmatched experience for both business and leisure tourists is at the heart of what we have to offer. Enjoy a beautiful setting while relaxing and rejuvenating in our fully equipped Spa & Wellness area. Our Hotel provides you with a peaceful haven, whether you are in town for a conference or to see Gdańsk's cultural riches.

We have taken great care to ensure that every aspect of our venue meets your demands. We promise a well-balanced combination of luxury and utility, from the elegantly sophisticated décor to the smooth incorporation of contemporary conveniences. Our Hotel tempts you with an appeal as distinct as you are, whether you're travelling for business, attending a conference, or just taking a relaxing break.

Hampton by Hilton Gdansk Old Town

- **Address: Lektykarska 4, Gdansk 80-831 Poland**
- **Hotel Class: 3-Star Hotel**
- **Price per day: $90**

A perfect combination of the past and current, the Hampton by Hilton Gdansk Old Town is situated in the centre of Gdansk's historic Old Town Square. The outside of the Hotel echoes the rich history around it with its ageless elegance of period architecture.

Once you're inside, a contemporary style is perfectly blended with a sanctuary of modern comfort. The sophisticated interior decor offers visitors a chic haven enhanced by cutting-edge facilities, signalling the designers' dedication to elegance.

Set in a prime location surrounded by cultural landmarks, the Hotel offers unparalleled accessibility to all of Gdansk's attractions. Everywhere you look, the city's historic charm is evident, from the famous Neptune Monument, which is just 180 meters away, to the Old Town's charming cobblestone alleyways.

With amenities to suit every demand, Hampton by Hilton Gdansk Old Town is the ideal destination for travellers seeking cultural immersion, business travellers visiting the neighbouring business sector, or shoppers wanting to indulge in local stores. From exciting local activities to the city's bustling tourist and retail areas, the Hotel acts as a portal to a tapestry of experiences.

Hotel Number One By Grano

- **Address: Jaglana 4, Gdansk 80-749 Poland**
- **Hotel Class: 3-Star Hotel**
- **Price per day: $83**

Number One Hotel is more than just a regular hotel; it's a unique sanctuary where consistency and harmony come together to provide for a really remarkable stay. Our senses serve as the compass that guides our memory as we travel the globe, identifying the impressions that stick with us. The goal of Number One Hotel is to become a beloved destination on your map, one that you will look forward to returning to and remembering with pure joy.

A symphony of sensory pleasures begins the minute you walk through our doors; every element has been painstakingly crafted to create an environment of unmatched comfort. Our dedication to maintaining consistency makes sure that each visit is a smooth continuation of the welcoming atmosphere from your last visit. Number One Hotel is a haven where all the little touches in our rooms, the delicious tastes in our dining areas, and the tranquil atmosphere all work together to produce an overwhelming sensation of well-being.

Ibb Hotel Gdańsk

- **Address: Ul. Długi Targ 14-16, Gdansk 80-828 Poland**
- **Hotel Class: 4-Star Hotel**
- **Price per day: $83**

Welcome to the centre of Gdansk, where our hotel calls with the promise of an immersive experience immersed in the rich cultural and historical fabric of the city. With 89 well-thought-out rooms—including family-friendly choices and those with breathtaking views of Długi Targ—we provide more than simply lodging; we provide a doorway to Gdansk's essence.

With a private balcony that offers a stunning view of the city, our Neptun apartment is the ultimate gem. Not only is it a room, but it's also a front-row ticket to the enthralling colour dance of the Gdansk cityscape.

In order to really comprehend Gdansk, even for a few while, you must immerse yourself in the city. Exiting our doors will immerse you in a thousand years of history just waiting to be discovered. The vivid colours of tenement buildings will surround you, the murmurs of recognized landmarks, and the energetic yells resonate through the streets.

Our interior designs are meant to complement rather than to distract. From the furnishings to the comfort of our mattresses, every aspect of our establishment is designed to provide you with the energy required to go on the journey that lies beyond our doors. Our Hotel turns into a refuge where the past and present blend together to flawlessly welcome you as you go out to explore Gdansk.

Qubus Hotel Gdansk

- **Address: Ul. Chmielna 47/52, Gdansk 80-748 Poland**
- **Hotel Class: 4-Star Hotel**
- **Price per day: $103**

Let me introduce you to a hidden treasure that embodies the ideal balance of modernism and tradition in Gdansk as you set off on your adventure: the Qubus Hotel Gdańsk. This luxurious sanctuary, which is tucked away along the lovely Motława River, effortlessly combines magnificence, stunning vistas, and an outstanding gastronomic experience.

The Qubus Hotel's remarkable contrast between its ancient heritage and modern elegance is evident from the minute you walk in. The building's height, which pays homage to Gdansk's legendary history, is evidence of the city's timeless appeal. Excitement grows as you rise, and the expansive panorama of the Motława River and the Old Town of Gdańsk appears before you. It is an image that will remain etched in your memory indefinitely.

Step into the well-thought-out rooms where comfort and modernity mingle. Every room is a symphony of fine details, providing an immersive experience in addition to a place to stay. Envision your hideaway overlooking the magnificent metropolis, surrounded by the temptation of broadband Internet, Wi-Fi, an LCD, satellite TV, a phone, and a radio.

A sumptuous breakfast awaits you each morning at the Qubus Hotel Gdańsk, filling your appetite and providing a visual feast of the river and Old Town. The Hotel goes above and beyond its opulent rooms to ensure your well-being. A state-of-the-art gym, sauna, and peaceful relaxation area are all part of the fitness facility, which welcomes you to unwind in between adventures.

And then there's the Restaurant, an alluring culinary symphony that promises fragrant treats, each course showcasing the area's culinary mastery. As you wait, the lobby bar beckons with its carefully chosen assortment of excellent wines and beverages, making it the ideal way to round off your days of sightseeing.

Hotel Gdańsk Boutique

- **Address: Szafarnia 9, Gdansk 80-755 Poland**
- **Hotel Class: 5-Star Hotel**
- **Price per day: $78**

Setting off for Gdansk reveals a hidden treasure, Hotel Gdansk, which perfectly captures the spirit of the city's maritime heritage and rich history. The Tricity's main Hotel, the carefully restored XVIIIth-century granary and the contemporary, nautically themed Yachting section come together to form a seamless and elegant whole.

Known for its charm, this boutique hotel is a shining star in the centre of Gdansk, tucked away by the lovely yacht port.

The Yachting section gives the interiors a modern touch while recalling the city's marine traditions, while the Granary radiates a timeless elegance that enchants guests with its historical enchantment.

The Spa at Hotel Gdansk is a contemporary haven of luxury, ranked among the most stylish on the Baltic coast and guaranteed to be one of Poland's best Med Spas. It is the ideal contrast to the bustling metropolis outside, providing a tranquil sanctuary.

Offering fine Polish and regional Gdansk cuisine, the Hotel's Restaurant is a gourmet paradise. A culinary adventure is in store, as each well-prepared dish captures the essence of the city.

CHAPTER 5: TOP ATTRACTIONS

Old Town Square

My trip took me to the Old Town Square, the vibrant centre of Gdansk, where I meandered through its charming lanes. This historical treasure turned out to be an intriguing crossroads of the past and present, located right in the middle of Gdansk's architectural wonders.

Finding your way to the Old Town Square is an adventure in and of itself. Every step you take will bring you closer to the centre of Gdansk's history, whether you approach via the busy Long Market or down the winding lanes dotted with amber stores.

A symphony of architectural genius is Old Town Square. As you approach St. Mary's Basilica, the grand façade with its elaborate Gothic features welcomes you. One example of the city's wealth during the Golden Age is the neighbouring Artus Court, a Renaissance masterpiece.

The Neptune Fountain, a well-known landmark in Gdansk, draws your eye as you go by. Admire the artistry and knowledge incorporated into this masterwork of the Renaissance. Gdansk's elegant Green Gate, representing the city's link to the royal path, beckons.

Don't overlook the undiscovered treasures nestled in the square's nooks as you explore. Explore quaint cafés where you can enjoy regional specialities and take in the lively ambience. Interact with regional artists who are showcasing their creations to give your encounter a more genuine feel.

As evening approaches, the Old Town Square changes, revealing a cosy light on the cobblestones. A distinct appeal emerges in the evening, when live music, street performers, and the soft murmur of conversation create an alluring atmosphere.

Start your adventure at the Golden Gate or the Long Market for a fully immersive experience. Discover stories of commerce, tenacity, and cultural diversity as you stroll about the plaza guided by the steady clatter of horse-drawn carriages.

Mary's Basilica

St. Mary's Basilica is a site that rises tall, echoing centuries of history and spiritual awe, as the early light warms the cobblestone streets of Gdansk. This Gothic-style building, known as the Queen of the Baltic, entices tourists with its lofty towers and opulence.

St. Mary's Basilica is tucked away in the centre of Gdansk's Old Town and is a lovely place to visit. Start your adventure at Old Town's great entryway, the Golden Gate. Wander around the little alleyways, where stories of a bygone past are spoken by ancient façade. With each step closer to the Long Market, the suspense grows as the towers of the Basilica become visible.

Enter St. Mary's Square and take in its expansiveness after passing through the commanding gate. The Basilica, with its elaborate front decorated with gargoyles and statues, rises ahead. Prior to going inside, pause to admire the Basilica's exquisite external elements, which serve as a precursor to its breathtaking interior.

The inside is darkly illuminated and greets you with a captivating display of stained glass, graceful arches, and elaborate ornaments. A feeling of heavenly grandeur is evoked by the nave's great height, which is topped by the astronomical clock. Don't miss the exquisitely carved wooden altar and the amazing astronomical clock, which is a marvel of medieval engineering.

Climbing to the top of the Basilica's tower provides breathtaking views over Gdansk for the daring. Climb the slender spiral staircase and see the city spread out below you as you ascend. A stunning view of the Baltic Sea, the flowing Motlawa River, and red roofs awaits you at the summit.

Gdansk Crane

The Gdansk Crane, a living monument that whispers stories of maritime grandeur and commerce that formed the city's fate, stands sentry along Gdansk's ancient waterfront. With its majestic silhouette against the captivating Motlawa

River, the Gdansk Crane is a fitting guide for you as you set off on your historical voyage.

Start your journey by meandering around Gdansk's Old Town's quaint cobblestone lanes. Most key attractions may be reached easily and picturesquely by foot from the Gdansk Crane, which is located close to the Old Town Square. To reach this nautical beauty, either follow the signs or let the city's architectural marvels lead the way.

Allow your senses to be enthralled as you get closer to the Gdansk Crane by the captivating design of the Green Gate and the captivating Neptune Fountain. Every step of the tour reveals a little bit of Gdansk's rich history, with the whole unfolding like a well-written drama.

The Gdansk Crane, a spectacular monument at the edge of the ocean, represents the city's strength in medieval trade. It was an essential instrument for loading and unloading goods from ships back in the 14th century, which cemented Gdansk's standing as a major maritime centre. Admire its enormous wooden construction, which is a monument to the era's technical prowess.

Reach the top of the crane's platform for a sweeping perspective over the river and the busy waterfront. Enter the crane and explore its interactive exhibitions, which will let you picture its historical importance and the flurry of activity that once surrounded it.

The Gdansk Crane is a living example of the city's resilience and marine tradition, not merely a historical relic. Imagine the many ships that once anchored here, bringing merchandise from far-off places and adding to the colourful mosaic of Gdansk's past as you stand in its shadow.

Westerplatte

With the Baltic Sea bathed in golden light, the little peninsula of Westerplatte rises out of the waves, ornamented with remnants of a forgotten past. Situated not far from Gdansk, this historic place represents bravery, defiance, and the unwavering spirit of the Polish people.

Take a boat from the dock in Gdansk and let the calm waters take you to Westerplatte to start your adventure. The brief journey envelops you in the serene splendour of the Baltic, setting the scene for the sad history that lies ahead.

The untamed nature of Westerplatte, dotted with the ruins of fortifications and the legends of those who bravely defended against overwhelming odds during the early stages of World War II, opens out as you disembark.

Continue, and you will see the Westerplatte Memorial, a solemn yet moving remembrance of the Polish defenders. The memorial, which is surrounded by vegetation and has a view of the ocean, is a moving reminder of the grit shown in the 1939 First World War Battle.

Examine the remnants of the guardhouse and barracks to see firsthand the unrelenting assaults that were sustained during the siege. Every stone has traces of history, providing a concrete link to the horrific events that took place on this sacred site.

The experience is enhanced by the Westerplatte Museum, which offers comprehensive historical insights into the peninsula. You are taken back in time to the crucial events that shaped Westerplatte's importance in Poland's wartime story via exhibits, images, and firsthand recollections.

Imagine the bravery of individuals who remained strong in the face of insurmountable obstacles as you stroll through the trenches and key sites. Every step is accompanied by the murmurs of history, prompting contemplation of the costs incurred in the name of liberty.

Climb to vantage spots high above the Baltic that previously saw the ebb and flow of history for expansive views of the water. The calm ocean bears quiet testimony to the tenacity contained in Westerplatte's soil.

Solidarity Centre

Wandering through Gdansk's old streets, you'll come upon the Solidarity Centre, a fascinating sight that echoes the strong pulse of a city that opposed persecution. This cultural landmark, which is tucked away amid the shipyards of Gdansk, is a journey into the moving story of Polish people's unwavering spirit, unity, and independence.

You may easily reach Gdansk's shipyards from the city centre to begin your dramatic adventure. The very earth under your feet whispers stories of workers' rights, demonstrations, and the beginning of a movement that rocked the foundations of an entire country as you approach the Solidarity Centre.

Enter the Solidarity Centre, and you'll be filled with the sounds of shipyard workers demanding change and the echoes of Lech Walesa's passionate speeches. The carefully chosen displays take you back to the stormy 1980s when political unrest was accompanied by the emergence of the Solidarity movement as a ray of hope.

See the famous Gate No. 2, which will live on in the history of Gdansk. Admire the Monument to the Fallen Shipyard Workers, a moving remembrance of those who gave their lives in defence of others. Experience hands-on exhibits, firsthand narratives, and artefacts that take you back to a period when solidarity was more than just an idea—it was a force to be reckoned with.

When you go through the Solidarity Center, stop at the Wall of Freedom. It is decorated with words that inspire hope and harmony. The BHP Hall, where important agreements were made, is a reminder of the extraordinary things that took place here.

The sound of history echoes as you leave the Solidarity Center. Give yourself a minute to process the enormity of the trip you've just completed—a pilgrimage into the centre of Gdansk's independence movement.

Oliwa Cathedral

A hidden treasure that beckons you to enter a world of architectural magnificence and serene spirituality is the Oliwa Cathedral, which you will discover as you stroll through Gdansk's picturesque cityscape. Nestled in the tranquil Oliwa Park, this majestic church is a reminder of centuries of artistic and historical achievement.

Start your magical adventure with a walk through Oliwa Park, a lush haven that prepares you for the breathtaking experience inside the cathedral. Alternatively, you may take a quick tram trip from Gdansk's city centre to the park's gate, where the cathedral stands gloriously.

The Oliwa church organ, one of Europe's biggest Baroque organs, enthrals your senses with its melodies as you approach the church. Prepare to be enthralled with the visual symphony that unfolds inside by following the melodic melodies that lead you through the finely carved wooden doors.

The baroque splendour of Oliwa Cathedral's interior is astounding. Admire the magnificent altars, elaborate murals, and elaborate ornaments that embellish the hallowed area. But without question, the pièce de résistance is the Oliwa Cathedral Organ, a 7,876-pipe musical marvel that has been vibrating since the 18th century.

Explore the area around the cathedral to find the calm Oliwa Abbey, an architectural wonder with its well-kept gardens and quiet cloisters. The serene surroundings provide an ideal counterpoint to the luxury of the cathedral's interior.

In addition to captivating audiences with its exquisite creative design, Oliwa Cathedral is a living example of how religion and culture can endure the test of time. Its distinctiveness stems from both its historical importance and the tasteful blending of surrounding buildings and the environment.

Gdansk Shipyards

Located beside the Motlawa River, the Gdansk Shipyards are more than simply a group of docks and cranes; they represent the vibrant centre of a city that has withstood many challenges throughout the ages. I could sense the echoes of freedom and camaraderie that radiated from this historic location as soon as I set foot on the shipyards' sacred grounds.

The colourful streets of the Old Town must be crossed in order to get to the Gdansk Shipyards. The trip itself is a tale, with each turn revealing a new aspect of Gdansk's fascinating past. The industrial silhouette of the shipyards will soon appear on the horizon as you follow the cobblestone roads and let the medieval facades lead you.

I felt as if I had travelled back in time to the 20th century when the shipyards had been the focal point of the

Solidarity movement. The imposing Gate No. 2 is a symbol of the labourers' tenacity and their struggle for fundamental human rights. The nearby European Solidarity Centre provides an in-depth history of this crucial time, replete with visually arresting displays and poignant first-person narratives.

It's like wandering through a living museum when you go through the shipyards. Overhead cranes tower above the city and rumours of shipbuilding might be murmured on the dry docks. Like a guardian of nautical history, the famous Gdansk Crane, an engineering wonder at the time, stands watch over the shipyards.

Travel from the Old Town to the European Solidarity Center by following the signs if you want to tour the Gdansk Shipyards. At the entryway are alternatives for guided tours and information on admission. Take in the interactive displays, and don't pass up the opportunity to scale the cranes for sweeping views of the city and the shipyards.

Amber Museum

The Amber Museum is a timeless gem located in the centre of Gdansk, encircled by the city's ancient Old Town. I set out on my adventure with the hope of unravelling the mysterious charm of the golden jewel, which drew me into a realm of natural splendour and historical significance.

The trip starts with you meandering through the Old Town's quaint lanes of Gdansk, and the Amber Museum appears next to the busy Long Market. Walking is the most convenient method to get there, and it lets you take in all of the medieval splendour of the city.

Entering the museum gives the impression of travelling back in time. The displays elegantly tell the narrative of amber, including everything from its prehistoric beginnings to its importance in the marine commerce of Gdansk. Carefully designed exhibits highlight the fascinating journey through amber's history and highlight the craftsmanship and cultural significance of this fascinating treasure.

Explore the hallways lined with antique amber objects, each of which narrates a story from a bygone era. Admire the exquisitely carved amber sculptures, which each perfectly capture the artistry of skilled artisans who turned unfinished amber into magnificent pieces of art. Amber's vivid colours, which range from warm honey tones to deep cognac tints, provide an eye-catching visual symphony that enthrals the senses.

The museum's replica of the fabled Amber Room, a missing masterpiece that formerly graced Russia's Catherine Palace, is its pièce de résistance. Admire the shimmering amber panels that are beautifully embellished with gold leaf, a stunning example of the artistry that has elevated amber to a treasured commodity throughout history.

Schedule a leisurely visit to the Amber Museum in order to thoroughly immerse yourself in the experience. Interact with the informed personnel to get a deeper understanding of each exhibit and this Baltic gem.

CHAPTER 6: CULTURAL EXPERIENCES

Museums and Galleries

European Solidarity Centre (ECS)

- **Address: Plac Solidarności 1, 80-325 Gdańsk, Poland**
- **Entry fee: PLN 32 (regular), PLN 24 (reduced), PLN 16 (children)**

The story of Gdansk comes to life as soon as you enter the European Solidarity Centre (ESC), resembling a striking display of bravery and tenacity. Standing at the exact core of where the Solidarity movement took root in 1980, permanently changing the course of Eastern Europe's history, I found myself enveloped in the echoes of a transformational age.

Daniel Libeskind's masterwork, the ECS, is much more than simply a museum—it's a dynamic representation of the unwavering courage of individuals who dared to oppose injustice. The building's remarkable architecture serves as a symbolic preamble to the powerful tales housed inside. Its strong lines and angles appear to capture the spirit of resistance and bravery that permeated the Gdansk Shipyards in those historic days.

Once inside, multimedia displays with flashing lights bring the exhibits to life, highlighting the ferocity of the battle and the victories of the Solidarity movement. The relics on exhibit take you back in time to a moment when a single shipyard became the epicentre of a revolution, each one bearing a unique weight of historical importance.

The exhibits' use of human tales really stood out to me. These were not far-off legends from another time; rather, they were the stories of people who bravely defied injustice and gave their everything for the sake of freedom. It serves as a moving reminder that history is more than simply a compilation of incidents; rather, it is a tapestry created from the goals and sacrifices of common people.

Museum of the Second World War

- **Address: Wały Jagiellońskie 2, 80-833 Gdańsk, Poland**
- **Entry fee: PLN 28 (regular), PLN 21 (reduced), PLN 14 (children)**

Welcome to the amazing voyage through the turbulent pages of history that rolled out between 1939 and 1945, which is the Museum of the Second World War. I couldn't help but be amazed at how this museum captures not just the story of World War II as a whole but also, more specifically, how deeply it affected Poland as I strolled through its hallowed corridors.

Envision entering what was once a Nazi munitions stockpile but was now a fount of wisdom and memory. The museum's complex intricacies are revealed like a vibrant tapestry, depicting a moment when the globe was engulfed in war mayhem. It is a living testament to the tenacity of a country, not just an assemblage of objects.

While painstakingly constructed dioramas take you back to the crucial events that determined the path of history, interactive exhibits invite you to immerse yourself in the tales of bravery and sacrifice. The story is real, a moving reminder of the resilience of the human spirit in the face of adversity.

With their quiet witnesses to the technical advancements in battle, the collection of military vehicles and weaponry provides a palpable link to the past. The memories of people who experienced the times are reflected in each exhibit, with Poland's story deftly linked to the larger picture of international struggle.

Main Town Hall - Museum of Gdansk

- **Address: Długi Targ 46/47, 80-833 Gdańsk, Poland**
- **Entry fee: PLN 25 (regular), PLN 18 (reduced), PLN 12 (children)**

The Main Town Hall in Gdańsk is so magnificent that you can't help but feel the centuries' worth of history being revealed to you. This Renaissance masterpiece is more than simply a structure; it is a dynamic representation of Gdańsk's past. Imagine passing through corridors where the city's medieval beginnings have been observed and where echoes of the past may still be heard.

Gdańsk's Main Town Hall welcomes you to explore its rich history with its complex façade and commanding presence.

The museum inside tells the fascinating tale of a city that grew from a little medieval village to a major hub of Hanseatic commerce as if the walls themselves could talk. Stories of thriving markets, maritime splendour, and the rich tapestry of Gdańsk's cultural and economic might will envelop you.

The displays provide a fascinating trip through time, with each antique representing a piece of the jigsaw that makes up the character of the city. The museum aptly captures this city's growth, from the ancient cobblestone alleys to the Hanseatic League's busy commercial port. You'll see how Gdańsk has evolved into a contemporary hub of culture and commerce as you walk through the exhibitions; it's a bustling place that skillfully unites its rich history with its dynamic present.

Museum of Amber - Museum of Gdansk

- **Address: Długi Targ 10, 80-833 Gdańsk, Poland**
- **Entry fee: PLN 20 (regular), PLN 15 (reduced), PLN 10 (children)**

Experience the fascinating world of amber at the Museum of Amber in Gdansk, which is aptly dubbed the "Amber Capital of the World." As someone who has seen the utter magnificence contained inside its walls, I take great pleasure in revealing the jewels that set this museum apart from the others.

These exhibitions bring to life Gdansk's rich history of amber mining and commerce, enthralling visitors with the fascinating narrative of the golden resin. The museum is home to one of the greatest collections of amber in the world, a captivating jumble that traces the history of this priceless stone from the earth's depths to the expert hands of craftspeople.

As you browse the displays, you'll be able to follow the paths taken by the amber trade routes that linked Gdansk with far-off places, bringing with them not just a jewel but also a little of the city's spirit. One is in awe of the artists who transformed raw amber into wearable art after seeing the display of exquisitely created items, amber jewellery, and breathtaking artworks.

National Maritime Museum

- **Address: Ołowianka 1, 80-832 Gdańsk, Poland**
- **Entry fee: PLN 25 (regular), PLN 18 (reduced), PLN 12 (children)**

Welcome to the National Nautical Museum of Gdansk, a nautical sanctuary tucked away on the lovely banks of the Motława River. I could feel the weight of history weighing on me as I stood in front of the ancient granary structure, now converted into a haven of maritime legends.

This museum tells the compelling story of Poland's nautical saga, making it a treasure trove for both maritime fans and curious tourists. The displays provide a smooth picture of Poland's nautical might, from the elegant Viking ships that formerly plied far-off seas to the enormous contemporary container ships that rule the seas today.

Entering the museum, you are greeted by an enchanting array of relics that all seem to whisper stories of ancient conquests and naval adventures. Marvel at the accuracy of the tiny reproductions that formerly navigated the Baltic waters, and lose yourself in the elaborate models that capture the majesty of sailing boats from decades ago.

The trip through the museum is a multi-sensory experience rather than just a visual one. The walls are covered with nautical paintings that evoke the spirit of Poland's maritime heritage, and the air is perfumed with the aroma of sea salt and the sounds of sailors' chants.

Theatres and Performing Arts

Theatres

Teatr Wybrzeże (The Coast Theatre)

Addresses:

- Main Stage: ul. Św. Ducha 2, 80-834 Gdańsk, Poland
- Scena Malarnia & Stara Apteka: ul. Teatralna 2, 80-834 Gdańsk, Poland
- Scena Kameralna: ul. 30 Bohaterów Monte Cassino Street, 81-759 Sopot, Poland

Let me tell you a story of cultural beauty as you stroll through the charming alleyways of Gdańsk's Old Town, which is centred by the oldest and most prominent theatre in the city—Teatr Wybrzeże, which is a tribute to Gdańsk's rich creative legacy. Imagine taking a trip into the realm of imagination and drama, where each show tells a fascinating story.

Tucked away in a landmark structure in the centre of the Old Town, Teatr Wybrzeże exudes a classic beauty. This theatre has been an important part of Gdańsk's cultural environment for many years, as if the stones that make up its construction are whispering stories from the past. The Main Stage, a theatrical treasure hidden inside the city's embrace, presents a repertory that alternates between cutting-edge international productions and timeless Polish classics.

However, Teatr Wybrzeże does not stick to the formula; instead, it spreads its creative wings across a number of stages, each serving as a blank canvas for more personal and experimental plays. This theatre's unique quality is its ability to combine innovation with history in a way that makes for a complex, above-average experience.

Szekspirowski Teatr Wybrzeże (Shakespearean Theatre)

- **Address: ul. Szafarnia 1, 80-835 Gdańsk, Poland**

Ah, let me describe for you a scene of pure theatrical magic: the Szekspirowski Teatr Wybrzeże, also known as the Shakespearean Theatre, is tucked away on the banks of the lovely Motława River. Imagine a granary from the 17th century that has been converted into a sanctuary for the works of the venerable William Shakespeare. The weathered bricks of the building reverberate with centuries of history.

You'll be taken to a realm where Shakespeare's beautiful poetry comes to life in the rich cadence of Polish as soon as you enter this cultural refuge. Anticipation permeates the air, and the atmosphere is thick with the Bard's centuries-old stories. It's a trip into the core of Shakespearean craftsmanship, not just a theatre production.

The Granary, with its rustic appeal and riverbank position, forms an intimate and dramatic background. The setting alone is a masterwork. The ageless plays are presented against the serene background of the Motława River, creating an atmosphere as if the ghosts of bygone eras had come together to watch them.

Experience something unique at the Szekspirowski Teatr Wybrzeże, regardless of your level of interest in the arts, whether you are an experienced Shakespearean or a casual spectator. Shakespeare's creative brilliance is brought to life for the audience as the passionate and accomplished performers bring the great stories to life.

Teatr Atelier

- **Address: ul. Jędrzejowska 20/21, 80-835 Gdańsk, Poland**

Welcome to the magical realm of Teatr Atelier, a little-known treasure in Gdansk's rich cultural history. Don't pass up the chance to take in the enthralling performances taking place within the cosy confines of Teatr Atelier as you stroll around the colourful streets of this ancient city.

This more intimate, independent theatre is a shining example of inventiveness, well-known for its provocative and inventive shows that stretch the bounds of creative expression. Imagine an environment where there is a buzz of excitement and every seat is a front-row pass to a world of ideas and feelings. Teatr Atelier is more than just a space; it's a doorway to a universe where plays from Poland and other countries effortlessly converge, captivating the audience.

Teatr Atelier is unique because of its dedication to variety. This vibrant venue presents events that go beyond the conventional boundaries of theatre, including dance, music, and multimedia art. The stage turns into a canvas, and every performance is a brushstroke, resulting in a work of art that cuts over language and cultural barriers.

Teatr Miniatura

- Address: ul. Ołowiana 13, 80-833 Gdańsk, Poland

Located in the centre of Gdansk, Teatr Miniatura is a hidden jewel that offers pleasure and joy to guests of all ages. Welcome to its fascinating universe. Imagine a warm, intimate theatre where colourful puppet figures come to life and captivate spectators with acts that push the bounds of the imagination.

Entering Teatr Miniatura, I was immediately thrust into a world where narrative was given a whole new meaning. This puppetry is an art form painstakingly designed to astonish and delight the viewer, not merely a means of amusement. You will be enthralled with the immersive experience that the presentations generate, which are geared toward different age groups.

Teatr Miniatura is unique because of its commitment to producing high-calibre plays. The puppet performances are visually arresting, but they also deftly combine dance and music, heightening the whole sensory experience. Every performance is a work of art, a symphony of colours and motions that is delightful to people of all languages.

Teatr Miniatura welcomes you with wide arms, whether you're a family with young children anticipating a fantastical voyage or a lone traveller looking for a unique cultural encounter. Every performance is a joyful shared experience between the audience and the puppeteers because of the venue's closeness.

Performing Arts

Baltic Sea Philharmonic

- **Address: ul. Ołowiana 1, 80-833 Gdańsk, Poland**

Imagine yourself in the centre of Gdansk, enthralled by the mesmerizing tunes that permeate the air as the sun sets, illuminating the sky in shades of orange and pink. Greetings from the Baltic Sea Philharmonic, a musical gem tucked away in this ancient city. I can attest that the magic is an experience that lasts beyond time, having personally experienced it.

The Baltic Sea Philharmonic, an ensemble that masterfully weaves a symphony of emotions through its numerous orchestral performances, is proudly hosted in Gdańsk.

Imagine a music hall that serves as both a venue and an architectural wonder, a contemporary testament to the city's support of the arts. The combination of amazing acoustics and modern architecture welcomed me as soon as I entered this aural paradise, laying the groundwork for an amazing musical experience.

This esteemed orchestra plays a varied repertoire of avant-garde works and classical classics all year round in Gdańsk. Every note in the music hall echoes with resonance, creating an atmosphere that is above and beyond the ordinary. The Baltic Sea Philharmonic invites you to immerse yourself in a soul-stirring symphonic experience, regardless of your level of familiarity with classical music.

Opera Nova

- **Address: ul. Długi Targ 38/40, 80-830 Gdańsk, Poland**

The Opera Nova shines as a cultural gem in the centre of Gdansk, luring you into a world of captivating performances that resonate with emotion and creative genius. I couldn't help but sense the tangible excitement of expectation as I stepped within the elaborate hallways of this beautiful opera house—a promise of an immersive experience that goes beyond the typical.

With its majesty and exquisite architecture, the Opera Nova is a symbol of Gdansk's dedication to the arts. Observing the city's thriving cultural landscape, I find myself enthralled with the variety of shows that take to its stages. The repertory offered here is nothing less than a captivating voyage across the world of performing arts, from the forceful crescendos of operas to the elegant pirouettes of ballets and the whimsical appeal of operettas.

Opera Nova is unique not just because of the variety of its shows but also because of its persistent dedication to quality. Every concert is a masterfully composed work of art that highlights the abilities of both local and international virtuosos. The Opera Nova experience is characterized by excellent quality and creative excellence, as seen by the thunderous acclaim that floods the auditorium after each performance.

Shakespeare Festival

The Shakespeare Festival, which takes place in the heart of Gdansk's ancient courtyards, is a mesmerizing show that takes you beyond space and time and into the Bard's universe. Imagine this: balmy summer afternoons, the light softly bathing old stones in a golden hue, and the fascinating rhythm of Shakespearean poetry filling the air. As someone who has personally experienced this cultural spectacle, I can confirm that the festival is a life-changing event that brings William Shakespeare's timeless words to life.

Each summer, the city's ancient building courtyards serve as the venue for this elaborate theatrical production. With the architectural treasures surrounding the audience adding to the performance's rich tapestry, the atmosphere is nothing short of breathtaking. It's more than just a play; it's an immersive experience where the elegance of Shakespeare's masterpieces blends with the echoes of history.

The event captures the exact essence of theatrical grandeur, whether it's the sorrow of Hamlet resonating against centuries-old walls or the hilarious fun of A Midsummer Night's Dream unfolding under the stars. The performers create an environment where the lines between the past and present are blurred as they move between tradition and innovation while dressed in historical costumes.

Music and Festivals

1. **Gdańsk Music Festival:** This classical music festival takes place in May and features performances by world-renowned orchestras and soloists.
2. **Open'er Festival:** This alternative rock and electronic music festival takes place in July and features headliners like Radiohead, Coldplay, and Kendrick Lamar.
3. **Mystic Festival:** This heavy metal festival takes place in June and features bands like Iron Maiden, Judas Priest, and Slayer.
4. **Salt Wave Festival:** This boutique festival takes place on the Hel Peninsula in August and features a mix of indie, rock, and electronic music.
5. **Tauron Life Festival:** This pop and rock festival takes place in August and features Polish and international artists.

Here are some tips for witnessing music and festivals in Gdansk as a visitor:

- Book your tickets in advance, especially for popular festivals.

- Be prepared for crowds, especially at the bigger festivals.
- Dress comfortably and for the weather.
- Ensure you have cash on hand, as some vendors may not be able to process credit card payments.
- Acquire fundamental Polish expressions, as they will facilitate communication with the residents.
- Most importantly, relax and have fun!

Local Cuisine and Culinary Experiences

Gdansk, Poland, is a treasure trove of culinary delights, blending traditional Polish fare with a modern twist and influences from its rich maritime history. Whether you're a seasoned foodie or just looking for a delicious adventure, Gdansk has something to tantalize your taste buds.

Must-Try Local Dishes

- **Pierogi:** These delectable dumplings, a Polish staple, come in a variety of fillings, from savoury (meat, potatoes, sauerkraut) to sweet (fruit, berries). Don't miss trying them at a local "pierogarnia" like Pierogarnia U Filusia, where they're made fresh daily.
- **Zapiekanka:** This open-faced toasted baguette is piled high with melted cheese, mushrooms, and other toppings, making it a perfect on-the-go snack or light lunch. You'll find zapiekanki vendors all over the city, especially near popular tourist spots.
- **Nalesniki:** These thin crepes are another versatile Polish dish, served with both sweet and savoury fillings. Try them with Nutella and bananas for a decadent treat, or go savoury with mushrooms and cheese.
- **Placki Ziemniaczane:** These potato pancakes are a crispy and comforting side dish or snack. Traditionally served with apple sauce or sour cream, they're a delicious way to experience Polish comfort food.

- **Zupa Grzybowa:** This hearty mushroom soup is a must-try for any soup lover. Made with a variety of wild mushrooms, it's the perfect way to warm up on a chilly day.

Beyond the Plate

- **Food Tours:** Immerse yourself in the Gdansk culinary scene with a guided food tour. These tours take you to hidden gems and local favourites, where you can sample a variety of traditional dishes and learn about the city's food culture.
- **Cooking Classes:** Get hands-on and learn how to make your Polish specialities. Cooking classes are a great way to bring home a souvenir and impress your friends with your newfound culinary skills.
- **Market Visits:** Explore the vibrant St. Dominic's Fair or smaller local markets to discover fresh produce, regional specialities, and handcrafted souvenirs. It's a great way to connect with the local community and find unique ingredients for your culinary creations.

Fine Dining

Gdansk also boasts a thriving fine dining scene, with restaurants offering modern interpretations of Polish cuisine and international flavours. For a special occasion, try Szafran, a Michelin-starred restaurant renowned for its innovative tasting menus.

Sweet Treats

No culinary adventure is complete without indulging in some sweet treats. Try a traditional "paczek," a deep-fried pastry filled with jam or fruit, or a "kremowka," a puff pastry filled with rich custard. For a taste of Gdansk's maritime heritage, don't miss the "marcepan," a delicious almond marzipan candy.

Gdansk's culinary scene is sure to satisfy any palate. So come hungry, be adventurous, and get ready to experience the flavours of this charming Polish city!

Here are some additional tips for planning your culinary adventure in Gdansk:

- **Try the local brews:** Gdansk has a growing craft beer scene, so be sure to sample some at a local brewery or beer bar.

- **Don't be afraid to ask for recommendations:** Locals are always happy to share their favourite spots to eat.
- **Bring your appetite:** Polish portions are generous, so come prepared to eat!
- **Relax and enjoy:** Food is a way to connect with culture and people, so slow down, savour the flavours, and make the most of your Gdansk culinary experience.

CHAPTER 7: SHOPPING IN GDANSK

Markets and Bazaars

For Foodies

Gdański Bazar Natury

- Address: Wały Jagiellońskie 80, 80-308 Gdańsk, Poland
- Opening Hours: Saturdays 9:00 AM - 3:00 PM, Thursdays 11:00 AM - 6:00 PM

Ah, let me take you on a lovely tour of the Gdański Bazar Natury, the centre of Gdansk's gastronomic essence. Imagine a bustling market area where the scent of locally grown, fresh food fills the air, and the booths are a visual and culinary feast, a rainbow of colour.

I was enthralled with the profusion of seasonal treasures as I strolled along the bustling aisles. The vibrant hues of sun-kissed fruits and a variety of veggies seemed to have been taken straight from the garden-filled stalls. The farmers proudly showed their abundant crops, their faces warmed by the sun, a monument to the rich agricultural tapestry that distinguishes Gdansk.

And the marvels of the food! Picture yourself biting into pierogi, the delicious dumplings made in Poland, with love and care. With every mouthful, your taste senses are treated to a ballet of heritage and a blast of flavours. Not only that, but vendors are selling a variety of baked products that would entice even the most self-controlling eaters, making the market a heaven for lovers of meat, cheese, and sweets.

I couldn't help but indulge in a zapiekanka, an open-faced sandwich topped with a unique assortment of toppings, while the sun shone on the outdoor market. It was a gastronomic masterwork that wonderfully captured the essence of Gdański Bazar Natury—a symphony of flavours and textures.

Green Market

- **Address: ul. Podwale Grodzkie 8/10, 80-838 Gdańsk, Poland**
- **Opening Hours: Daily 6:30 AM - 4:00 PM**

Enter the Green Market, the centre of Gdansk's thriving food scene, where both residents and tourists will find a sensory feast thanks to the lively kiosks and busy ambience. I can vouch for the fact that this covered market is more than simply a place to shop—it's an enthralling experience that envelops you in the spirit of the city—having seen its vibrant tapestry firsthand.

Fresh food meets local charm at the Green Market, a gourmet delight with a vibrant atmosphere and eye-catching displays. Imagine a food enthusiast's dream come true: rows of booths decorated with a variety of freshly caught seafood, tender pieces of meat, and seasonal veggies. The symphony of scents that permeate the air invites you to discover the wide range of sensations that Gdansk has to offer.

However, it goes beyond groceries. The market is a veritable gold mine of regional culture, with sellers selling anything from handcrafted trinkets that encapsulate the essence of Gdansk to aromatic flowers. You can't help but be lured to the booths offering deliciously prepared dishes as you go down the aisles; this is the ideal chance to try real Polish cuisine that has been lovingly and expertly prepared.

Nicholas Market

- **Address: Targ Św. Mikołaja, 80-833 Gdańsk, Poland**
- **Opening Hours: Daily 10:00 AM - 10:00 PM**

The St. Nicholas Market offers a magical experience as soon as you enter the center of Gdansk. Imagine a bustling market square filled with vendors offering mouthwatering smells of traditional Polish cuisine. I can't resist telling you about the colourful stories that are being told in this quaint setting while I watch this gastronomic extravaganza.

The market square is a visual and gastronomic feast, a kaleidoscope of hues and sensations. The focus is on traditional Polish cuisine, such as the mouthwatering fragrance of grilled kielbasa drifting through the air and pierogi overflowing with flavorful contents. Every booth seems to narrate a tale of culinary artistry transmitted throughout several generations, beckoning you to savour the genuine flavour of Poland.

St. Nicholas Market's delicious blend of foreign and local cuisine is what makes it unique. Explore the booths to discover a world of cuisines right in front of you. This market square has everything you could want for your palate, from the unusual tastes of different cuisines to the cosy warmth of traditional Polish soups.

Cosy cafés and welcoming eateries tempt you to stay a bit longer in the busy market. Choose a cosy location, enjoy your selected treats, and take in the lively ambience. It's an exploration of Gdansk's rich cultural heritage, not simply a meal.

For Shopaholics

Dominikan Flea Market

- **Address: ul. Dominikańskiego 5, 80-832 Gdańsk, Poland**
- **Opening Hours: Sundays 10:00 AM - 3:00 PM**

Explore Gdansk's undiscovered treasures, and you'll come across the fascinating Dominikan Flea Market, which is a veritable rainbow of antique treasures just waiting to be discovered. Imagine a bustling market tucked away in Old Town's charming historic district, where every turn leads to another fascinating story and a unique assortment of treasures.

Allow me to vividly describe the Dominikan Flea Market for you as a witness to its liveliness. The smell of antiquity permeates the air, and your curiosity is piqued by the ancient furniture, classic clothes racks, and worn bookshelves in some of the booths. It is more than simply a market—it's an odyssey into the past and an outdoor museum filled with treasured memories and long-forgotten artefacts.

You'll find more than just tangible goods as you meander through the maze-like booths; every item has a backstory. Antique furniture has the patina of numerous discussions; vinyl recordings whisper songs of ancient times, and antique clothes tell stories of beautiful soirées. Every object in the immersive experience has the potential to become a piece of history unique to you as the past and present dance together.

Amber Sky

- **Address: Długi Targ 36/38, 80-836 Gdańsk, Poland**
- **Opening Hours: Daily 10:00 AM - 7:00 PM**

The Amber Sky is a location that shimmers with a bright appeal of its own as the sun sets over Gdansk, bathing the city in a warm amber light. Imagine a busy market with kiosks displaying amber, the valuable gemstone of the area.

I was surrounded by a rainbow of hues and the delightful aroma of handcrafted goods.

Nestled in Gdansk, The Amber Sky is a treasure trove that calls with the promise of exquisite and one-of-a-kind jewellery. Observing the market's charm, I couldn't help but be pulled to booths featuring understated but exquisite jewellery that perfectly encapsulated the golden wealth of the Baltic Sea. Bracelets murmured stories of skill passed down through the years. They were exquisitely made and meticulously fashioned.

There is an amazing selection of rings and earrings available on the market for individuals looking for more than simply jewellery. With amber that has withstood the test of time and tide and washed ashore as a gift from the sea, each piece seems to retain a little of Gdansk's past. The diversity is striking; some pieces have a sophisticated brilliance, while others have a rustic appeal, demonstrating the treasured gemstone's adaptability.

Long Market

- Address: Długi Targ, 80-830 Gdańsk, Poland
- Opening Hours: Shops and stalls vary, generally open late morning to evening

Ahh, the magical charm of Gdansk's Long Market, a busy thoroughfare that crisscrosses the Old Town like a colourful ribbon of exploration. Envision a bustling promenade filled with a variety of stores and kiosks, all of which promise a wealth of surprises for curious travellers such as yourself.

The joy of exploration filled the air as I walked down the cobblestone walkway. The kiosks drew my attention with their items, a kaleidoscope of souvenirs, clothes, amber jewellery, and traditional Polish crafts, all clothed in hues that reflected the city's rich past. I felt as if the street itself was calling me to participate in Gdansk's living history by whispering stories of the artists who painstakingly created these masterpieces.

The experience of strolling through the vibrant environment of the Long Market adds to its allure, in addition to its products. This lively boulevard offers something for everyone, regardless of your level of experience or if you're simply in the mood for some leisurely window browsing. Every shop exudes a symphony of colours and textures that engage the senses, reflecting the rhythm of local life.

For a Local Experience
Oliwa Market

- **Address: ul. Opata Jacka Rybińskiego 26, 80-303 Gdańsk, Poland**
- **Opening Hours: Daily 7:00 AM - 7:00 PM**

The Oliwa Market is a wonderful refuge that you shouldn't miss as you walk through Gdansk's picturesque alleyways. This undiscovered treasure, nestled away from the busy tourist attractions, reveals the vibrant everyday lives of the people who live in Gdansk. Imagine a bustling market square filled with colourful flowers, the freshest vegetables possible, and all the necessities that make up the fabric of everyday life in the area.

It seems as if you are entering the beating heart of the city of Gdansk as you stroll through Oliwa Market. I can speak to the realism that permeates every aspect of this vibrant scene as a witness. The air is filled with the perfume of ripe fruits and vibrant blossoms, and locals converse animatedly, their smiles as warm as the sun-soaked vegetables.

Each booth is a kaleidoscope of hues and textures, just waiting for you to explore. The market is a sensory extravaganza, offering everything from crunchy veggies to aromatic herbs. It is more than simply a place to buy; it is a vibrant theatre of everyday life, with interactions between customers and sellers pulsating the pulse of Gdansk.

Dominic's Fair

- **Location varies yearly, typically in Gdansk Główny Railway Station and surrounding areas**
- **Dates: July & August (specific dates vary)**

Ah, allow me to take you on a tour through the centre of the lively cultural tapestry of Gdansk, where the aroma of nostalgia and the sounds of tradition fill the air. A vibrant celebration of the spirit of Polish culture, St. Dominic's Fair takes place in the city in July and August. Imagine Gdansk's Old Town's cobblestone streets turned into a rainbow of hues and noises that invite you to take part in the celebrations.

I can attest that St. Dominic's Fair is a spectacular event that you shouldn't miss. The captivating variety of booths at the fairgrounds, each filled with treasures that narrate tales of bygone eras, brings the grounds to life. Polish cuisine will entice your palate with dishes like flavour-filled pierogi and savoury grilled sausages. Explore the booths filled with elaborate crafts and souvenirs, each one a unique creation that reflects the rich history of this charming city.

The sound of live music fills the streets with excitement and celebration, becoming the beating heart of St. Dominic's Fair. Folk dances spread infectious energy throughout the air, and talented performers enthral audiences with traditional songs.

You're likely to discover a market or bazaar in Gdansk that you'll adore, regardless of your hobbies. To begin exploring, put on your walking shoes!

Here are some additional tips for exploring markets and bazaars in Gdansk:

- **Bring cash:** Many vendors at markets and bazaars do not accept credit cards.
- **Be prepared to bargain:** It's common to bargain at markets and bazaars in Poland. Don't be afraid to haggle a bit to get a good price.

- **Learn a few basic Polish phrases:** A few simple phrases like "dziękuję" (thank you) and "proszę" (please) will go a long way.
- **Be patient:** Markets and bazaars can be crowded and chaotic. Take your time and enjoy the experience.

Unique Souvenirs

Gdansk, Poland, is a charming city with a rich history and culture, making it a perfect destination for a unique souvenir. Here are some ideas for souvenirs that you won't find anywhere else:

1. **Amber:** Gdansk is known as the "Amber Capital of the World," so it's no surprise that amber is a popular souvenir. This fossilized resin comes in a variety of colours and can be found in everything from jewellery and ornaments to chess pieces and sculptures. There are even shops that sell amber-infused coffee and vodka!
2. **Goldwasser liqueur:** This sweet and spicy liqueur is made with 20 different herbs and spices and contains flakes of 22-karat gold. It's a truly unique souvenir that will impress your friends and family.

3. **Kaszubian embroidery:** The Kashubians are a Pomeranian ethnic group with a rich cultural heritage. Their traditional embroidery is colourful and intricate, and it can be found on everything from tablecloths and pillowcases to jackets and handbags.
4. **Danziger Goldwasser:** This traditional liqueur is made with saffron, cloves, cinnamon, and other spices. It's a bit sweeter than Goldwasser and has a more floral flavour.
5. **Stained glass:** Gdansk is home to some of the most beautiful stained glass in Europe. You can buy small pieces of stained glass or even larger panels to take home with you.
6. **Handmade pottery:** Gdansk has a long tradition of pottery making. You can find beautiful hand-painted ceramics in all shapes and sizes.
7. **Music boxes:** Gdansk is also known for its music boxes. These beautifully crafted boxes come in all sizes and play a variety of tunes.

No matter what your interests are, you're sure to find a unique souvenir in Gdansk. With its rich history and culture, this city has something for everyone.

Here are some additional tips for finding unique souvenirs in Gdansk:

- **Shop at local markets:** The best place to find unique souvenirs is often at local markets. Here, you'll find a wide variety of handmade items from local artisans.
- **Avoid tourist traps:** The shops in the main tourist areas will tend to have the same souvenirs that you can find anywhere else. If you're looking for something unique, head off the beaten path.
- **Ask the locals:** The locals are always a great source of information on where to find the best souvenirs. They may know of some hidden gems that you wouldn't find on your own.
- **Haggle:** It's perfectly acceptable to haggle over prices in Poland. So don't be afraid to bargain for a better deal.

Fashion and Local Design

Gdansk, Poland, is a city with a rich history and culture, and its fashion scene is no exception. In recent years, there has been a growing trend of local designers emerging, creating unique and stylish pieces that reflect the city's character.

Here are some of the things that make Gdansk fashion special:

- **Inspiration from the Baltic Sea:** The Baltic Sea is a major influence on Gdansk fashion, with designers using colours, textures, and patterns that evoke the sea, sand, and sky. For example, the brand Zoya uses flowing silks and linen in shades of blue and green, while local jewellery designer Martyna Majewska creates pieces inspired by seashells and seaweed.
- **Focus on craftsmanship:** Gdansk has a long tradition of craftsmanship, and this is reflected in the quality of local fashion. Many designers use natural materials and traditional techniques to create unique and long-lasting pieces. For example, the brand Leśniewski uses locally sourced wool to

create knitwear, while the shoemaker Patryk Wowczyk handcrafts leather boots and shoes.
- **Sustainable and ethical practices:** Many local designers are committed to sustainable and ethical practices. They use organic materials, upcycle vintage clothing, and produce their garments in small batches to minimize waste. For example, the brand Uroda uses recycled cotton and linen to create its clothing, while the lingerie brand Milagro uses fair trade certified organic cotton.
- **A mix of styles:** Gdansk fashion is not limited to any one style. There is something for everyone, from avant-garde to minimalist, bohemian to classic. This makes it a great place to find unique and stylish pieces that express your style.

If you're interested in exploring Gdansk fashion, here are a few tips:
- Visit the many local boutiques and concept stores, such as Seeyou, La Mania, and Elska.
- Attend one of the city's many fashion events, such as the Amber Fashion Week or the Gdansk Fashion Days.

- Follow local designers on social media to stay up-to-date on their latest collections.
- Gdansk fashion is a vibrant and exciting scene, and it's definitely worth checking out if you're looking for something unique and stylish.

Shopping Districts

1. **Forum Gdańsk** is the newest and largest shopping centre in Gdansk. It is located in the city centre, near the Old Town. The centre has over 220 shops, cafes, and restaurants, as well as a cinema. The design of Forum Gdańsk is modern and sleek, with a glass and steel facade.
2. **Galeria Bałtycka** is another popular shopping centre in Gdansk. It is located in the Wrzeszcz district, not far from the main train station. The centre has over 200 shops, restaurants, and service outlets. The design of Galeria Bałtycka is more traditional, with a red brick facade and a clock tower.
3. **Ulica Dluga (Long Street)** is a historic street in the Old Town of Gdansk. It is lined with shops, cafes, and restaurants, as well as many historic buildings.

The street is cobbled and pedestrian-only, making it a popular place to stroll and do some shopping.

4. **Mariacka Street** is another historic street in the Old Town of Gdansk. It is known for its amber shops, which sell amber jewellery and other amber products. The avenue is adorned with various coffee shops and dining establishments.

5. **Targ Węglowy (Coal Market)** is a square in the Old Town of Gdansk. It is a popular place to buy souvenirs, such as amber jewellery, traditional Polish pottery, and wooden crafts. The square is also lined with cafes and restaurants.

6. **Designer Outlet Gdańsk** is an outlet mall located outside of Gdansk. It is home to over 100 stores, including Adidas, Nike, Calvin Klein, and Guess. The mall is designed to look like a seaside fishing village, with a lighthouse and cobblestone streets.

CHAPTER 8: NIGHTLIFE AND ENTERTAINMENT

Bars and Pubs

Winston Bar

Address: ul. Piwna 5/7, Gdańsk, Poland

Opening Hours:

- **Sunday - Thursday: 4:00 PM - 2:00 AM**
- **Friday - Saturday: 4:00 PM - 3:00 AM**

Winston Bar is a haven where well-made cocktails transform into an immersive experience for the senses, a monument to the art of mixology. Imagine yourself surrounded by modern furnishings and bathed in a cosy, welcoming light that creates the ideal atmosphere for an indulgent evening. The bartenders at Winston are like real alchemists; they transform alcoholic beverages into artistic creations with a charming and captivating flare.

However, Winston Bar is a haven for anyone looking for a lively environment and more than simply a place to get drinks. A spirit of unity filled the room as I delighted in the cheerful banter between locals and other tourists. The contagious laughing and clinking drinks created an image of an environment where relationships are formed with ease.

The soulful sounds of live music fill the air on weekends at Winston, making them very unique. You may picture yourself enjoying a well-mixed beverage as the mellow music fills the bar. The atmosphere is just amazing; it's a masterful fusion of tastes and noises that make for an experience that cannot be compared.

Pub Red Light

Address: ul. Długa 72/73, Gdańsk, Poland
Opening Hours:

- **Sunday - Thursday: 12:00 PM - 2:00 AM**
- **Friday - Saturday: 12:00 PM - 3:00 AM**

Pub Red Light's atmosphere is a harmonious blend of old-world charm and modern sophistication. You're taken to a bygone period as you settle into the soft red velvet, where tales are told over pints of fine beers and handcrafted drinks. This collection showcases both worldwide classics and hidden treasures from Gdansk's eclectic brewing scene. The antique memorabilia adorning the exposed brick walls creates an intimate ambience ideal for enjoying the company and the beverages. Pub Red Light offers a sensory voyage through liquid pleasures, catering to all palates, whether you're a lover of cocktails or beer.

Match your beverage with the delicious pub meal that is served, which has a fascinating blend of regional and global influences. Every meal, from flavorful nibbles to substantial burgers, pairs well with the wide selection of beverages.

U Szkota

Address: ul. Szeroka 36/37, Gdańsk, Poland

Opening Hours:

- **The operational hours are from Sunday to Thursday, spanning from 12:00 PM to 1:00 AM.**
- **Friday - Saturday: 12:00 PM - 2:00 AM**

Well, allow me to introduce you to a hidden treasure that lies in the centre of Gdansk: U Szkota, a classic Irish bar that exists outside of space and time. I can confirm that U Szkota is more than simply a bar; it's a thriving establishment and a cultural landmark that welcomes both residents and visitors with open arms. I am a living example of Gdansk's dynamic heartbeat.

Imagine this: as soon as you walk through the door, a joyful wave welcomes you as if you were an old friend. Not merely a bar, U Szkota is a vibrant living example of friendship and the happiness that comes from spending time with others. The vibrant conversation of visitors exchanging stories about their travels across Gdansk and the laughing of the residents create an electrifying environment.

U Szkota's weekly live music routine creates a musical tapestry that adds to the pub's charm. Irish folk music, with its heartfelt songs or modern hits and their upbeat rhythms, creates a musical atmosphere that unites the varied groups of people gathered inside these sacred walls.

Let's also discuss libations. With its extensive collection of Guinness and other Irish beers, U Szkota guarantees that every drink will transport you to the green island. True masters of their trade, the bartenders contribute to the friendliness that characterizes this Gdansk tradition by pouring with accuracy and a genuine grin.

Labeerynt Craft Beer Pub

Address: ul. Szafarnia 11, Gdańsk, Poland

Opening Hours:

- **The operational hours are from 2:00 PM to 12:00 AM, Sunday through Thursday.**
- **Friday - Saturday: 2:00 PM - 2:00 AM**

Oh, allow me to tell you about the Labeerynt Craft Beer Pub, a haven for beer connoisseurs located in the centre of Gdansk. Upon entering this sanctuary of hops and brews, your senses are instantly piqued by the heady perfume of many craft beers, both domestic and foreign.

Envision a warm, well-lit area with timber details and an enticing ambience that matches the wide assortment of options. With more than 30 taps, Labeerynt offers an amazing selection that promises to take you on a tasty and diversified trip through the world of craft beer. Polish brewers' artistry and the appeal of foreign beers to a worldwide audience are shown on the taps.

The staff of beer experts at Labeerynt who lead you through this aqueous maze is what really makes it unique. They help you navigate the myriad of alternatives with enthusiasm and expertise, making sure your pint precisely matches your palate. The knowledge of the staff turns your choice into an experience, regardless of your level of beer expertise.

Nightclubs

Klub Miasto Aniołow (Angels' City Club)

- Address: ul. Szafranowa 1, 80-834 Gdańsk, Poland

Enter Klub Miasto Aniołow, a mysterious place where the sound of music echoes through the old walls of a former monastery. This evocative club is more than just a place to go; it's an adventure through space and time. Imagine yourself surrounded by the hip-hop, R&B, house, and techno beats that permeate the atmosphere—a demonstration of the club's dedication to providing a wide range of musical experiences.

The scene is mesmerizing; several dance floors entice you to immerse yourself in the music, with each beat echoing the history etched in the surrounding stones. Enter the large beer garden as night falls to find a place of fun and quality time spent with loved ones outside. The VIP section is waiting for anyone looking for a more special experience; it provides a haven for those who want a little more seclusion.

Sassy CLUB

- **Address: ul. Długi Targ 33/34, 80-835 Gdańsk, Poland**

Welcome to the legendary Sassy CLUB, the beating core of Gdansk's nightlife. This chic retreat, tucked away in the Old Town's enchanted embrace, calls to the adventurous spirits looking for a night to remember. Imagine yourself among the cobblestone streets, where Sassy CLUB, a ray of enthusiasm and vitality, combines the best elements of the past with the present.

I can confirm that Sassy CLUB is the place where the young and fashionable of the city go to have a good time, having seen the exciting evenings that take place within its walls. The thundering sounds that pour out into the cobblestone streets produce an electrifying atmosphere. As soon as you walk in, the sleek, contemporary décor welcomes you with a large dance floor that begs for unrestrained celebration.

The VIP section is a haven for people looking for a more personal encounter; it radiates exclusivity. The cocktail bar, an epicentre of inventiveness, creates sophisticated but powerful concoctions to make sure your evening goes as smoothly as the beat that pulses from the speakers.

House and techno sound rule supreme at Sassy CLUB, generating an enticing magnetic draw for music lovers. It's a musical refuge. Now and again, live DJ performances electrify the atmosphere and turn the night into a symphony of unique sounds.

The Parlament Music Club

- **Address: ul. Piwna 34/35, 80-835 Gdańsk, Poland**

Here, at The Parlament Music Club, the city's rhythms burst to life in a symphony of beats and melodies - the beating heart of Gdansk nightlife. This iconic bar, which is alive with energy and rich in history, has been a ray of amusement for more than thirty years, solidifying its place in Gdansk culture.

Let me build a picture of the wonder that lies ahead of you as a witness to the colourful stories weaved inside these walls. There are three levels in the club, and each has a different vibe to fit the mood of the patrons. With pop, rock, and techno music pulsing through the air, the main floor calls with an alluring invitation to dance. Locals and tourists alike are present in this vibrant group, giving in to the contagious rhythms that reverberate throughout the night.

Head upstairs to the second story, where you'll discover a calm haven. For those looking for a more laid-back atmosphere, a lounge area offers a cosy haven. A cocktail bar encourages you to enjoy beautifully created beverages. Before heading upstairs to the third story, where the beauty of live music emerges, this is the ideal diversion. Watch as regional and international musicians hit the stage, their performances generating a unique symphony that reverberates right down to the club's core.

Pub Torpeda

- **Address: ul. Szafranowa 7, 80-834 Gdańsk, Poland**

Ah, allow me to take you to the centre of the lively nightlife of Gdansk, where the laughing reverberates throughout the night, and the energy is infectious. Imagine yourself in Pub Torpeda, a welcoming sanctuary that draws in both residents and interested tourists. As soon as you walk in, a buzz of excitement fills the air, and the vibrant environment becomes your nighttime partner.

For beer lovers, the selection of beers on tap at Pub Torpeda is a symphony. The collection takes you on a tour through the brewing arts, from regional crafts to trendy drinks from throughout the world. The dance floor transforms into a painting as the evening goes on, where unplanned happiness takes centre stage. The enticing rhythms and the contagious rhythm of laughing serve as the perfect backdrop for newly formed connections.

Live music brings the stage to life, resulting in an immersive experience that perfectly encapsulates the vibrant spirit of Gdansk. It's more than simply a bar—it's a gathering place for tales, a patchwork of many faces joining together in the exuberant celebration of life.

Hi-Fi High Five

- **Address: ul. Mariacka 39, 80-837 Gdańsk, Poland**

Welcome to the Hi-Fi High Five bar, a hidden treasure of Gdansk's nightlife that invites you to take a nostalgic trip back in time to the enchanted 1950s. Nestled away from the busy crowd, this distinctive institution is proof of the diverse character of the city. I can't help but share the absolute delight of discovering this nostalgic refuge as a witness to its charm.

Enter, and you'll be immersed in a different period, with antique furniture all about you whispering history. A unique musical experience is created by the carefully chosen recordings that line the walls. Melodies of jazz and swing fill the air, evoking a captivating ambience that is yet exuberant and relaxed.

Hi-Fi High Five isn't simply a throwback place; the sporadic DJ sets give it a modern spin, making it a vibrant environment that welcomes the merging of old and new. It's the ideal place to relax, have a drink, and immerse yourself in the chic atmosphere. This unconventional bar guarantees an evening of enjoyment for anyone looking for a change of pace. Every note and every sip is a celebration of the colourful spirit of Gdansk. Go off the main path and let Hi-Fi High Five create a lasting impression on your trip through Gdansk.

Live Music Venues

1. **B90:** This former Gdansk Shipyard canteen is now a renowned live music club, hosting international

and local bands across genres. The industrial ambience adds to the unique experience.

2. **Klub Muzyczny Parlament:** A long-standing institution in the city's Old Town, Parlament features three floors with different vibes. The main stage hosts established Polish and international acts, while the smaller Studio caters to up-and-coming artists.

3. **Ulica Elektryków:** This street in the Wrzeszcz district is a hub for alternative music, with several venues like Bunkier, Drizzly Grizzly, and Elektryczny Żuraw offering gigs by local and international indie bands, DJs, and electronic music acts.

4. **SASSY:** If you're looking for something a bit more intimate, SASSY is a cosy bar with a focus on jazz, blues, and soul music. They also host jam sessions and open mic nights.

5. **Craft Cocktails:** This cocktail bar doubles as a live music venue, showcasing local singer-songwriters and acoustic acts in a relaxed setting.

Here are some additional tips for planning your live music exploration:

- Check online listings and event calendars to see what's happening during your visit.
- Don't be afraid to venture outside the Old Town; some of the best venues are located in other districts.
- Seek advice from the locals; they will gladly divulge their preferred places.
- Be prepared to pay a cover charge at some venues, especially for bigger shows.
- Most importantly, relax and enjoy the music!

CHAPTER 9: DAY TRIPS FROM GDANSK

Sopot

Amidst the historical beauty of Gdansk, Sopot tucked away along the Baltic Sea, beckons as the ideal day trip destination. I embarked on a seaside excursion that promised not just a change of scenery but also a symphony of sensations waiting to be discovered as the sun said farewell to the cobblestone alleys of Old Town.

When we boarded the train from Gdansk, the ride turned into an enchanted preamble to the adventure that day. The clickety-clack of the beat spoke to the expectation of what was to come. Panoramic vistas that heightened the sensation of wanderlust were revealed via windows framing breathtaking sights of the Baltic shore.

Entering Sopot's platform was like stepping into another universe, one where the vibrant talk of visitors and locals blended harmoniously with the sound of breaking waves and the aroma of the sea. With its graceful pier and colourful promenade, Sopot seemed picture-perfect in my mind.

The longest wooden pier in Europe, Sopot Pier gracefully reached out into the Baltic. Every stride seemed to be a rhythmic communion with the waves, a dance with the water. A murmur of laughing could be heard from the assortment of eateries bordering the pier as seagulls flew above.

Stumbling down Monte Cassino Street into the centre of Sopot, I came into a culinary paradise. Polish and foreign food was delightfully available at charming cafés and restaurants. The feast turned into a crucial component of the voyage, bringing tastes that reflected Sopot's multifaceted beauty at intervals throughout the day.

A leisurely walk in the lush Spa Park offered a peaceful diversion from the bustling streets. A feeling of tranquillity was conveyed by the whispering air and the majestic trees that created a canopy above. In the middle of the bustling seaside area, the park provided a tranquil haven with its lovely walks and secret nooks.

Seeing the peculiar phenomenon known as the Crooked House is a must-do while visiting Sopot. Its fanciful building perfectly captured the spirit of Sopot's playfulness, seeming to defy gravity. I descended to the shore, where golden beaches extended to the horizon, beckoning me to have a refreshing swim in the Baltic or sunbathe.

I took the train back to Gdansk as the sun started to set, illuminating the horizon with pink and gold tones. Not only had the day excursion to Sopot provided a change of scenery, but it had also been a sensory symphony, a masterful fusion of nature, history, and seaside charm. As dusk was falling, I thought about how special Sopot was and resolved to visit its alluring beaches again. My day vacation in Gdansk became an odyssey of coastal beauties, forever altered by the day's crescendo of discovery.

Gdynia

Day travel from Gdansk to Gdynia is an expedition along the Baltic Sea, where every turn reveals a new aspect of the region's natural splendour. My journey started as the sun said farewell to Gdansk's cobblestone alleyways, promising a day filled with discovery and nautical wonders.

Gdynia's promenade along the sea stretched out like a beautiful painting, welcoming me with wide arms. As I strolled along the Baltic Cliff, the expansive vistas of the turquoise water captivated me. The sea aroma wafted through the cold wind, energizing, like a preview to the glories of the sea ahead.

The Gdynia Maritime Museum, a veritable gold mine of naval history, was the highlight of my day. From interactive exhibitions to historic warships, the museum skillfully combined interest and information. I felt a link to the naval history of Gdynia as I stood in front of the tall ships.

Oksywie Pier called out for a seafood feast with its quaint restaurants. Lunch turned into a gourmet celebration of Gdynia's marine culture, complete with the catch of the day and a view of bobbing boats.

The cliffside hike at Orłowo was a peaceful diversion. Wandering amid verdant foliage, the cliffs revealed stunning views of the Baltic. It was a time to reflect quietly and take a break from the bustle of the city.

The port of Gdynia, a thriving hub of maritime activity, provided an insight into the city's economic life. I was astounded by the port's smooth transition into the city as I saw yachts and cargo ships living in harmony with one another.

The day was ending sweetly when I found myself surrounded by neoclassical buildings in Kościuszko Square. The area was transformed into a painting of golden colours by the warm illumination of the setting sun. It was the ideal way to cap off a day full of amazing marine experiences.

Getting about Gdynia was easy because of the effective public transit system in the city. I was able to make the most of my time by connecting major sights with trains and buses. Interacting with the kind natives enhanced my trip positively.

Explore the coastal symphony of Gdynia, from the serene clifftop setting of Orłowo to the marine museum's echoes of nautical legends. This day excursion was more than simply a travel across geography; it was an exploration of a city where culture and the sea coexist together. The waves appeared to whisper stories of an enduring relationship between land and water as I said goodbye to Gdynia. Set off on this voyage, follow the wind of the sea, and discover the marine treasures that Gdynia has to offer.

Malbork Castle

Gdansk is glistening with the morning light, and a visit to Malbork Castle during the day adds a magical touch to your investigation of this Polish treasure. Just a short ride from the ancient alleys of Gdansk, be ready for an experience that will take you beyond time to the medieval enchantment of Malbork Castle.

As I boarded the train from Gdansk, I could feel the excitement building, knowing that the train would take me to the biggest brick castle in the world. My anticipation for what was coming increased as I took in the stunning scenery of the Polish countryside on the comfortable trip.

As soon as I got off the train, I was struck by how majestic Malbork Castle was—its tall walls conjuring images of years past. Travelling to the castle is an experience in and of itself as you pass through a quaint village that seems to be stuck in time on cobblestone streets.

I gasped when the massive silhouette of the castle filled my vision. Malbork Castle's immense size and elaborate Gothic architecture take you back to a time when legends were created, and knights roamed the land. I was astounded by the painstakingly kept rooms, each of which echoed stories of medieval grandeur, and I learned about the rich past of the Teutonic Knights while exploring the castle's interiors.

Malbork Castle is unique because of its dedication to a rich narrative. You can picture life inside the castle's walls thanks to the interactive exhibitions that bring history to life. Every aspect of this place begs to be explored, from the armoury with its clinking armour to the Grand Master's home furnished with antique furnishings.

As soon as I stepped inside the castle's expansive courtyard, a symphony of historical echoes engulfed me. Here, the sheer size of the castle's architectural design really mesmerizes. There's a tangible feeling of wonder when you stand under the imposing walls, which is a monument to the technical marvel that is Malbork Castle.

To really enjoy your day excursion, go there early to beat the crowds and take advantage of guided tours to learn about the secret history of the castle. Enjoy the audio tours that reveal the mysteries of this medieval masterpiece, and don't forget to wear comfortable shoes for wandering the vast grounds.

A day spent at Malbork Castle is an immersive experience with the luxury of a bygone age, not merely a historical tour. As the day draws to a conclusion and you say goodbye to this architectural wonder, the sounds of ages past and the echoes of knights reverberate, giving you a deep appreciation for the magical trip from Gdansk to the centre of medieval grandeur.

Kashubian Switzerland

Take a day excursion from Gdansk to Kashubian, Switzerland, and you'll enter a world straight out of a storybook, one that stays with you long after the day is over. Glittering lakes and beautiful surroundings surround the area. My senses were buzzing with excitement as I left Gdansk in hopes of discovering this undiscovered treasure.

With undulating hills and meadows that appeared to dance in time with the light wind, the route to Kashubian Switzerland unfurled before me like a lovely ribbon. A journey unlike any other was framed by the lush surroundings, which created an ideal painting.

As the "Land of a Thousand Lakes," Kashubia is well-named, and every piece of water we came across had a certain allure of its own. Every find, from secret lakes that resembled something out of a fantasy book to quiet reflections that mirrored the nearby woodlands, was a peaceful haven just waiting to be discovered.

In this backdrop of untamed beauty, typical Kashubian villages appeared, their wooden huts painted with bright flower designs. The tour was enhanced with a deeper cultural resonance by the residents' warm hospitality as they told stories of Kashubian folklore.

My passion for hiking was satiated by the abundance of paths in Kashubian Switzerland, which led to sweeping vistas that showcased the amazing grandeur of the area. Walking through the Wdzydze Kiszewskie open-air museum or standing atop Wiezyca, the tallest hill in the region, seemed like a communion with history and nature.

Enjoying the regional cuisine is a must-do on every trip. Rugged inns beckoned in Kashubia, with filling specialities such as Kaszëbskô Kôładka (Kashubian soup) and pierogi stuffed with woodland mushrooms. With every mouthful, the abundant agricultural produce of the area was honoured gastronomically.

Travelling in Kashubian Switzerland calls for a balance of adventure and pragmatism due to its large size. My enjoyment of the scenery was uninterrupted by the information offered by amiable residents and local guides.

This day excursion included stops at alluring locations, including as the ethereal Swornegacie floating town and the mysterious Czocha Castle. The spirit of a location where time appeared to stand still was caught in every shot, not simply the surroundings.

I was struck, as always, by the deep connection I felt to this magical place as the sun sank below the horizon, casting the Kashubian sky in shades of orange and lavender. Visits to Kashubian Switzerland during the day are more than simply travels—they're encounters with the natural world, cultural customs, and the unfathomable beauty that characterize the environs of Gdansk. Let Kashubia enchant you and make your Gdansk journey unforgettable if you're looking for a day that goes above and beyond the norm.

CHAPTER 10: OUTDOOR ACTIVITIES

Beaches and Waterfront

Gdansk boasts stunning beaches and a charming waterfront, offering visitors a variety of ways to soak up the Baltic Sea atmosphere. Here are some recommended selections to explore:

Beaches

- **Brzeźno Beach:** This lively beach is closest to Gdansk's Old Town, making it a convenient choice for city explorers. Enjoy soft sand, shallow waters, a bustling promenade lined with shops and eateries, and even a historic pier.
- **Jelitkowo Beach:** A short hop from Sopot, Jelitkowo offers a more peaceful escape with a wide sandy shoreline and calmer waters. It's popular among families and those seeking a relaxed beach experience.
- **Stogi Beach:** This long stretch of sandy beach is a favourite among locals. Enjoy sunbathing, swimming, windsurfing, or simply strolling along the scenic coast. You'll also find some beach bars and restaurants here.
- **Sobieszewo Beach:** Located on a picturesque island near Gdansk, Sobieszewo Beach boasts pristine, untouched beauty with dunes, nature reserves, and frequent amber finds. It's ideal for nature lovers and those seeking a secluded escape.

Waterfront

- **Gdansk Old Town:** Take a scenic stroll along the Motlawa River in Gdansk's Old Town. Admire the colourful Hanseatic architecture, historic bridges, and bustling ports. You can also hop on a boat tour for a different perspective of the city.
- **Westerplatte Peninsula:** This historic peninsula played a crucial role in World War II. Explore the WWII museum, wander along the scenic beaches, and soak up the panoramic Baltic Sea views.
- **Gdansk Shipyard:** Visit the European Solidarity Centre at the Gdansk Shipyard, a symbol of Poland's fight for freedom during communism. Learn about the Solidarity movement and its impact on Polish history.

Remember, Gdansk's beaches can get crowded during peak season (summer months). If you prefer a quieter experience, consider visiting in the shoulder seasons (spring and autumn).

No matter what your preferences are, Gdansk's beaches and waterfront offer something for everyone. So grab your swimsuit, sunscreen, and sense of adventure, and get ready to explore!

Parks and Gardens

Oliwa Park

- **Address: Opata Jacka Rybińskiego 27, 80-333 Gdańsk, Poland**
- **Entry Fee: Free**

Oliwa Park is a vast green space tucked away in the heart of Gdansk, whispering stories of Gothic magnificence and peace. Oliwa Park's tranquillity unfurled like a tale just waiting to be discovered as I strolled over its vast grounds. Reaching the magnificent Oliwa Cathedral, a Gothic masterpiece that captivates the spirit with its exquisite design, was made possible by towering trees that provided a leafy canopy and dappling sunlight on well-trodden walkways.

This is more than simply a park—it's a sanctuary of breathtaking scenery and rich history. Oliwa Cathedral, with its lofty spires and historic elegance, is a symbol of the city's rich past. An amazing visual feast surrounded me as I wandered around the park, the soft melody of singing birds and the sound of rustling leaves creating a symphony.

Enjoy the little joys in life in Oliwa Park by setting up a picnic blanket under the shade of the old trees, taking a leisurely bike ride along its winding pathways, or taking a tranquil stroll to enjoy the fresh air. Oliwa Park is the biggest park in Gdansk and a living example of the city's dedication to protecting the natural world, its history, and the pure delight of discovery. Around every turn, a new aspect of this enchanted haven is revealed.

Majdanek Park

- **Address: ul. Długi Targ 46/47, 80-830 Gdańsk, Poland**
- **Entry Fee: Free**

Wandering through the centre of Gdansk, you'll come onto Majdanek Park, a beloved sanctuary for residents and curious tourists alike. Tucked away in the heart of the city, this charming park is a mosaic of peace and ethnic diversity. Imagine bright greenery, gentle leaf rustling, and children's laughing mingling with the bustle of city life.

Majdanek Park is a live example of the spirit of Gdansk, more than merely a park with trees and walkways. You'll come across a variety of sculptures and monuments along the walkways that each tell a tale of the tenacity and legacy of the city. The park skillfully blends the old with the new, creating an environment that inspires introspection and admiration.

Families will find the park to be a playground haven where kids' happy cries mix with the happy tweets of birds soaring above. A little café tucked away in the foliage provides a tranquil place to relax, have a coffee, and take in the tranquil atmosphere.

Orunski Park

- **Address: Podwale Staromiejskie 1, 80-831 Gdańsk, Poland**
- **Entry Fee: Free**

Orunski Park, tucked away along the lovely banks of the Motlawa River, is a hidden treasure in Gdansk that welcomes you to enjoy the beauty of the city in a peaceful environment. I can personally vouch for its charm and the magical experience that is waiting for you within this lush haven. As you meander around the park, the alluring cityscape of Gdansk will surround you, providing a wide-angle view of breathtaking architectural feats.

The embracing of history in Orunski Park is what really sets it apart. Historic structures stand tall and proudly among the verdant surroundings, each telling a story from a bygone period. The Granaries whisper tales of trade and commerce that once flourished along the riverbanks behind their aged facades. An iconic focal point that lends a sense of grandeur and evokes the spirit of marine stories and ancient mythology is the Neptune Fountain.

Jelitkowo Park

- **Address: Park Jelitkowski, 80-336 Gdańsk, Poland**
- **Entry Fee: Free**

Jelitkowo Park is a coastal sanctuary that beckons you into its embrace of sun-soaked pleasure and aquatic delights. It is tucked away along the serene beaches of Gdansk Bay. This park is more than simply a green haven; I can personally speak to the pure happiness that exists there as a symphony of leisure and the natural world.

Imagine walking along the colourful paths of the park as the soft sea wind fills you with the energizing aroma of the Baltic Sea. Jelitkowo Park welcomes you with open arms and provides a serene environment for those who like adventure as well as those who seek calm. The bay stretches out before you like an azure canvas, beckoning swimmers to cool down in its soothing embrace and providing a haven for sun worshippers along the sandy shoreline.

The park becomes a windsurfing playground with multicoloured sails dancing against the horizon for those looking for an adrenaline rush. The stunning sights around you are the only thing that can compare to the adrenaline of windsurfing.

With a variety of eateries and cafés sprinkled around the coastline, Jelitkowo Park reveals its gastronomic delights as the day goes on. Savour regional cuisine over a leisurely supper while taking in the captivating views of the bay.

Ujazd Park

- **Address: ul. Uczniowska 22, 80-289 Gdańsk, Poland**
- **Entry Fee: Free**

While meandering around the quaint Wrzeszcz neighbourhood in Gdansk, I came onto Ujazd Park, a peaceful haven tucked away from the bustle of the city. This lush sanctuary is the ideal getaway from the busy city life, attracting both nature lovers and thrill seekers. Ujazd Park is more than simply a park; it's a haven where the gentle murmurs of nature coexist peacefully with the beat of the city.

I felt peaceful as I strolled along the meandering paths, which was a pleasant diversion from the daily grind. Charming lakes and ponds dot the park's vast grounds, lending an air of magic to the surroundings. The well-maintained trails made for a joyful voyage of discovery for hikers and bikers, with each bend unveiling a fresh view of breathtaking scenery.

Ujazd Park has something for everyone, whether you're a casual biker enjoying the soft wind or an enthusiastic hiker enjoying the difficulty of the paths. The calming waters, vivid vegetation, and clean air all combine to create a calming atmosphere.

Boating and Water Sports

Ah, Gdansk! It's a beautiful city with stunning architecture and, as you've correctly identified, some fantastic opportunities for boating and water sports. Whether you're a seasoned sailor or a curious first-timer, Gdansk has something for everyone on the water.

Here are some ideas to get you started:

Boat Tours

- **Sightseeing cruises:** Glide along the Motlawa River and admire the charming Old Town, historic gates, and iconic sights like the Grune Tor (Green Gate) and the Golden Gate. Several companies offer different cruise options, some even with eco-friendly electric boats.
- **Canal tours:** Experience a different perspective of Gdansk by venturing into the picturesque canals. Kayak tours are a great option for a more interactive experience, allowing you to explore hidden spots inaccessible to larger boats.

Water Sports

- **Kayaking and canoeing:** Explore the waterways at your own pace, perfect for both solo adventurers and small groups. Beginners can choose guided tours, while experienced paddlers can rent equipment and venture further.
- **Stand-up paddleboarding (SUP):** Enjoy a low-impact workout while soaking in the city views. SUP boards are relatively easy to learn and offer a unique way to navigate the river.
- **Sailing:** If you're feeling adventurous, try your hand at sailing on the Baltic Sea. Several operators offer sailing lessons and charters tailored to all skill levels.

Other options

- **Windsurfing and kitesurfing:** For thrill-seekers, Gdansk Bay offers excellent conditions for wind-powered water sports. Lessons and equipment rentals are available, but be sure to check weather conditions before heading out.
- **Fishing:** Fishing enthusiasts can cast their lines in the Motlawa River or head out to sea for a deeper

water experience. Several companies offer fishing charters with experienced guides.

Tips for planning your Gdansk water adventure:

- **Consider the time of year:** Gdansk's boating season typically runs from spring to autumn, with the most pleasant weather in summer. However, if you're looking for quieter experiences, spring or autumn might be better options.
- **Check weather conditions:** Wind and waves can quickly change on the Baltic Sea, so always check the forecast before heading out on the water.
- **Book in advance:** Popular tours and activities can fill up quickly, especially during peak season. Consider booking online or contacting operators directly to secure your spot.
- **Choose the right activity for your skills and fitness level:** Be honest with yourself about your experience and comfort level when choosing an activity. Don't be afraid to ask for help or guidance from instructors or operators.

With its charming canals, historic waterfront, and access to the Baltic Sea, Gdansk is a haven for water enthusiasts. I hope this information helps you plan your perfect Gdansk boating or water sports adventure!

Hiking and Nature Trails

1. **Oliwa Park:** This expansive park encompasses centuries-old olive trees, a historic Cistercian monastery, and several hiking trails. The Łapalice trail leads through the forest to a picturesque waterfall, while the Oruński Stream trail offers a peaceful riverside walk.
2. **Głowica Hill:** Located within Oliwa Park, Głowica Hill provides stunning panoramic views of the Tricity region, including Gdańsk, Sopot, and Brzeźno. Ascending to the summit may pose some challenges, yet the payoff justifies the exertion.
3. **Ścieżka Cecylii:** This charming coastal path winds its way from Brzeźno to Jelitkowo, offering breathtaking views of the Baltic Sea and the Gdansk Bay. Along the way, you'll pass sandy beaches, rocky cliffs, and charming seaside cottages.
4. **Reagan Park:** Located on the eastern side of Gdańsk, Reagan Park is a popular spot for hiking, cycling, and picnicking. The park features a

network of trails that wind through forests, meadows, and wetlands.

5. **Tricity Landscape Park:** This vast protected area encompasses forests, hills, lakes, and rivers. The park offers a variety of hiking trails, ranging from easy to challenging, with plenty of opportunities to spot wildlife.

Here are some additional tips for planning your hike:

- Select a trail that aligns with both your fitness level and prior hiking experience.
- Make sure to don appropriate attire and suitable footwear.
- Bring plenty of water and snacks.
- Let someone know your rencana and expected return time.
- Be respectful of the environment and wildlife.

CHAPTER 11: PRACTICAL INFORMATION

Emergency Contacts

General Emergencies

- **European Emergency Number:** 112 (works from any phone, even without a SIM card)
- **Police:** 997
- **Ambulance:** 998
- **Fire Brigade:** 999

Tourist-Specific

- **Tourist Emergency Helpline:** +48 22 278 77 77 or +48 608 599 999 (English-speaking operators)

Hospitals

- **University Clinical Hospital:** Nowe Ogrody 2, +48 58 764 01 16 (open 24 hours)
- **City Hospital:** ul. Smęczyńska 35, +48 58 345 67 00 (open 24 hours)
- **Emergency Medical Care:** Nowe Ogrody 1-6, +48 58 301 05 14 (open 24 hours)

Other Useful Numbers

- **Taxi:** +48 58 196 66
- **Airport Information:** +48 58 301 82 00
- **Gdansk Tourist Information:** +48 58 301 77 55

Additional Tips:

- Download the "112 Polska" app for emergency information and location sharing.
- Save the above numbers to your phone or write them down on a piece of paper.
- Familiarize yourself with your surroundings and know where the nearest emergency exits are.
- If you don't speak Polish, try to learn a few basic phrases, such as "pomocy" (help) and "nie rozumiem" (I don't understand).

Remember: In case of an emergency, stay calm and clearly communicate the situation and your location.

Healthcare and Safety

Gdansk generally enjoys a good reputation for both healthcare and safety, offering visitors and residents alike a comfortable and secure environment. Here is an overview of what you can anticipate:

Healthcare

- **Public Healthcare:** Poland has a universal healthcare system funded through taxes. EU citizens can access public healthcare services at no cost with their European Health Insurance Card (EHIC). Others may need to pay. Public hospitals and clinics are generally well-equipped, though wait times can sometimes be longer than in private facilities.
- **Private Healthcare:** Private clinics and hospitals are readily available and offer shorter wait times and advanced medical technologies. The costs are lower compared to Western Europe but still higher than the public system. English is often spoken in private clinics.
- **Pharmacies:** Pharmacies ("Apteka") are plentiful and well-stocked with prescription and over-the-

counter medication. Pharmacists can offer basic medical advice for minor ailments.

Safety

- **General Safety:** Gdansk is considered a safe city with a low crime rate. Petty theft and pickpocketing can occur, particularly in crowded areas, so take standard precautions like keeping valuables secure.
- **Traffic Safety:** Road traffic can be busy, especially during peak hours. Be aware of crosswalks and pedestrian lights. Zebra crossings are not automatic right-of-way for pedestrians.
- **Emergency Services:** The emergency number in Poland is 112 for ambulances, fire brigades, and the police. English-speaking operators are not always available, so consider learning basic Polish phrases for urgent situations.

Remember:

- While tap water is generally safe to drink in Gdansk, some people prefer bottled water.
- Air quality can sometimes be a concern, especially during winter months. If air quality is compromised, it is advisable to consider the use of a mask.

- Always check current travel advisories from your home country before your trip.

Wi-Fi and Connectivity

Gdańsk, a beautiful city in northern Poland, boasts excellent Wi-Fi and connectivity options, making it easy for visitors and residents to stay connected. Here is an overview of what you can anticipate:

Free Wi-Fi

- **GD@ŃSKwifi:** The city of Gdańsk offers a free public Wi-Fi network called GD@ŃSKwifi, with over 100 hotspots throughout the city centre, including the Old Town, parks, and public buildings. The network is open and easy to connect to, requiring only acceptance of the terms of use. You can find hotspot locations on a map available on the GD@ŃSKwifi website.
- **Cafes, restaurants, and bars:** Many cafes, restaurants, and bars in Gdańsk offer free Wi-Fi for their patrons. This is a great option if you're looking for a place to relax and enjoy a coffee or meal while staying connected.

Mobile data

- **Polish mobile operators:** All major Polish mobile operators, such as Orange, Play, Plus, and T-Mobile, offer mobile data plans with coverage throughout Gdańsk. You can purchase a SIM card with a data plan at one of their stores or online.
- **International roaming:** If you're travelling from abroad, your mobile operator may offer roaming data packages for Poland. These can be expensive, so it's worth checking the rates before you travel.

Other options

- **Eduroam:** If you're a student or faculty member at a university, you can connect to the Eduroam network, which is available at universities and research institutions around the world.
- **Hotels and apartments:** Most hotels and apartments in Gdańsk offer Wi-Fi for their guests. Typically, this is incorporated within the cost of the accommodation.

Here are some additional tips for staying connected in Gdańsk:

- Download a Wi-Fi map app before you travel, such as WiFi Map or Google Maps. These apps can help you find Wi-Fi hotspots near you.
- Carry a portable power bank to keep your devices charged while you're on the go.
- Be aware of your data usage, especially if you're using mobile data. Roaming charges can be expensive.

With its extensive Wi-Fi network and reliable mobile data coverage, Gdańsk makes it easy for everyone to stay connected while exploring this charming Polish city. So, pack your laptop or smartphone and get ready to experience the better of Gdańsk, both online and offline!

Local Laws and Customs

Gdansk, a beautiful port city in Poland, offers a captivating blend of history, culture, and modern charm. While Polish laws and general etiquette apply, Gdansk also has its unique local customs and traditions that visitors should be aware of to ensure a smooth and enjoyable experience.

Laws and Regulations

- **Public Drinking:** While Poland has a liberal attitude towards alcohol, public drinking is frowned upon, especially near historical monuments or churches. Drinking beer in outdoor areas like parks is usually acceptable, but avoid excessive drunkenness.

- **Smoking:** Smoking indoors is prohibited in public places like restaurants, bars, and public transportation. Designated smoking zones are commonly provided in outdoor areas.

- **Traffic Rules:** Gdansk follows right-hand driving. Crosswalks are designated for pedestrians, and it's crucial to give way to them. Public transportation is efficient and affordable, so consider using it instead of driving.

- **Waste Disposal:** Be mindful of littering and properly dispose of trash in designated bins. Recycling is encouraged, with separate bins for different materials.

Customs and Etiquette

- **Greetings:** Poles generally greet each other with a handshake and a nod. Addressing elders or strangers with "pan" (Mr.) or "pani" (Ms.) followed by their surname is the norm.
- **Tipping:** Tipping is not mandatory but is appreciated in restaurants and cabs. A small tip of around 10% is customary.
- **Dress Code:** Gdansk residents dress casually but neatly. Avoid overly revealing clothing in religious or conservative settings.
- **Queueing:** Poles line up for their turn in queues. Respect your place and avoid cutting in line.
- **Church Visits:** When visiting churches, dress modestly and be respectful of religious practices. Avoid talking loudly or taking photos inside.
- **Local Delicacies:** Gdansk boasts delicious seafood and traditional Polish cuisine. Try local specialities

like pierogi (dumplings) and kaszubski gulasz (stew).

Additional Tips:

- Learn some basic Polish phrases like "dzień dobry" (good day) and "dziękuję" (thank you).
- Carry currency in zloty (PLN), as not all places accept euros or credit cards.
- Gdansk is a walkable city, so pack comfortable shoes.
- Visit the local Tourist Information Office for maps, recommendations, and cultural events.

CHAPTER 12: LOCAL EVENTS AND FESTIVALS

Annual Events Calendar

Winter

- **St. Dominic's Fair (Jarmark św. Dominika):** A lively 3-week street fair in Gdansk's Old Town featuring arts and crafts, live music, and traditional food. Takes place in July (dates vary).
- **Gdansk Shakespeare Festival:** International and Polish theatre companies perform traditional and experimental versions of Shakespeare's plays. Accompanied by concerts and a parade. Held in August (dates vary).
- **FETA:** An international street theatre festival with jugglers, mimes, stilt walkers, dancers, and storytellers from around the world. Takes place in July (dates vary).
- **Christmas Markets:** Gdansk's Old Town transforms into a winter wonderland with charming wooden stalls selling traditional festive food,

decorations, and handicrafts. Opens in late November to late December.

Spring

- **Baltic Sail:** An international sailing regatta with hundreds of boats participating in races on the Baltic Sea. Held in June (dates vary).
- **Amber Run:** A charity run/walk through Gdansk's Old Town raising funds for children's cancer treatment. Takes place in April (dates vary).

Summer

- **Neptune Day (Dzień Neptuna):** A colourful parade and water festival celebrating the city's maritime heritage. Held in June (dates vary).
- **Open'er Festival:** One of Poland's biggest music festivals, featuring international and Polish bands across various genres. Takes place in July (dates vary).
- **St. Dominic's Fair (Jarmark św. Dominika):** Mentioned above.

Autumn

- **International Kite Festival:** The sky above Gdansk fills with colourful kites of all shapes and sizes. Held in September (dates vary).
- **Gdansk Marathon:** A challenging marathon race through the city's scenic streets. Takes place in October (dates vary).

CHAPTER 13: SUSTAINABLE TRAVEL TIPS

Eco-Friendly Practices

Sustainable Transportation

- **Tramp or Bike:** Gdansk is a compact city, perfect for exploring on foot or by bike. Rent a bike from one of the numerous rental shops and cycle along the scenic Motlawa River or through the charming Old Town. Consider joining a guided bike tour for a deeper appreciation of the city's history and culture.
- **Public Transport:** Gdansk boasts an efficient tram and bus network, making it easy to get around without a car. Purchase a Gdansk City Card for unlimited travel on public transport and discounts on attractions.
- **Water Taxis:** Take a scenic water taxi ride across the Motlawa River for a unique perspective of the city. Choose eco-friendly companies that use electric or hybrid boats.

Eco-Conscious Dining

- **Support Local and Organic:** Seek out restaurants that source their ingredients locally and prioritize organic produce. This helps minimize the ecological footprint associated with the transportation of food and promotes the livelihoods of local farmers.
- **Vegetarian/Vegan Options:** Gdansk offers a growing selection of vegetarian and vegan restaurants, perfect for those seeking a lighter footprint. These options often utilize local, seasonal ingredients and minimize food waste.
- **Mindful Consumption:** Avoid food waste by ordering only what you can finish and opting for smaller portions if unsure.

Responsible Sightseeing

- **Respect Green Spaces:** Gdansk has numerous parks and gardens, perfect for relaxing and enjoying nature. Stick to designated paths, avoid littering, and appreciate the local flora and fauna.
- **Choose Eco-Friendly Tours:** Opt for walking tours or bike tours led by local guides who are passionate

about sustainability. They can share insights into Gdansk's green initiatives and hidden eco-gems.
- **Minimize Souvenirs:** Resist the urge to buy unnecessary souvenirs that may end up unused or discarded. Instead, choose locally crafted items made from sustainable materials or donate to a local environmental organization.

Additional Tips:

- **Carry a Reusable Water Bottle and Shopping Bag:** Avoid single-use plastics by carrying your own water bottle and shopping bag.
- **Choose Eco-Friendly Accommodations:** Stay in hotels or guesthouses committed to sustainability practices like energy efficiency and water conservation.
- **Learn Basic Polish Phrases:** Knowing a few Polish phrases like "dziękuję" (thank you) and "proszę" (please) can encourage communication with locals and foster a more responsible cultural exchange.

Responsible Tourism Initiatives

Environmentally friendly practices

- **Green spaces and active travel:** Gdansk boasts expansive green spaces like Park Oliwski and Jelitkowo Beach, perfect for eco-friendly activities like cycling and hiking. The city also invests in cycling infrastructure and promotes car-free zones to reduce emissions.
- **Sustainable water management:** The city prioritizes water conservation through rainwater harvesting and greywater systems in public buildings.
- **Waste reduction and recycling:** Gdansk implements waste separation programs and promotes reusable shopping bags to minimize waste generation.

Supporting local communities

- **So Stay Hotel:** This unique hotel employs young people from foster care, providing them with training and job opportunities in the hospitality industry.

- **Local food and crafts:** Gdansk encourages tourists to patronize local markets and restaurants to support traditional food producers and artisans.
- **Cultural experiences:** Immerse yourself in Gdansk's rich history and culture through guided tours led by local experts. Visit the European Solidarity Centre to learn about the city's role in the Solidarity movement, or explore the charming Old Town to discover its architectural gems.

Responsible wildlife tourism

- **Wildlife watching:** Opt for boat tours that prioritize responsible whale and dolphin watching practices to minimize disturbance to these magnificent creatures.
- **Supporting conservation efforts:** Consider volunteering with local organizations working to protect Gdansk's natural environment and endangered species.

Choosing eco-friendly accommodation

- Look for hotels with sustainability certifications, like Green Globe or EcoHotels.

- Choose smaller, locally owned guesthouses or B&Bs that often have a smaller environmental footprint and support the local community.

CONCLUSION

As you reach the final pages of this Gdansk travel guide, I extend my heartfelt gratitude to you for choosing this companion on your journey through the captivating city of Gdansk. Your exploration of this Baltic gem is a testament to your adventurous spirit, and I trust that the pages of this guide have added value to your travel experience.

Gdansk, with its rich history, cultural tapestry, and vibrant ambience, has undoubtedly left an indelible mark on your travel memories. From the medieval allure of the Old Town to the echoes of solidarity in the shipyards, each chapter unfolded a different facet of Gdansk's allure. The city's resilience through centuries, evident in its reconstructed landmarks post-World War II, resonates with the spirit of renewal that defines Gdansk today.

Our journey has taken us through the historic Old Town Square, the maritime grandeur of St. Mary's Basilica, the symbolic Gdansk Shipyards, and the serene retreat of Ujazd Park. We've explored the cultural treasures in museums, indulged in the vibrant nightlife, and savoured the flavours of traditional Polish cuisine. Day trips to Sopot and Gdynia offered glimpses into the diverse landscape surrounding Gdansk, enhancing the depth of our exploration.

As you venture into the city, I hope you've found joy in every step, discovering the blend of medieval charm and modern vibrancy that defines Gdansk. Whether you've marvelled at the Gothic architecture, revelled in the lively atmosphere of Long Market, or simply enjoyed a moment of serenity by the Baltic Sea, Gdansk has undoubtedly left an indelible mark on your heart.

This guidebook aimed to be your trusted companion, providing practical insights, cultural context, and hidden gems to ensure your Gdansk experience was nothing short of extraordinary. Remember, travel is not just about the places you visit; it's about the stories you collect, the connections you make, and the moments that become timeless.

As you bid farewell to Gdansk, may the memories linger, and may the city's spirit accompany you on your future journeys. Gdansk, with its maritime tales, amber-lit streets, and welcoming embrace, will forever be a chapter in your travel story.

Once again, thank you for allowing this guide to be part of your travel adventure. Wishing you secure journeys, and may your explorations consistently be marked by awe and new findings.

Printed in Great Britain
by Amazon